UNAFRAID

A SURVIVOR'S QUEST FOR HUMAN CONNECTION

BY NIYATI TAMASKAR

Tamaskar,
Jun 2021

This book is a memoir. It reflects the author's present recollections
of experiences that occurred in the past. Some names and identifying
characteristics have been changed, some events have been compressed, and
some dialogue has been recreated.

This book is not intended as a substitute for the medical advice
of physicians. The reader should consult a physician in matters
relating to his/her health.

Paperback ISBN: 978-1-7332245-1-2
Ebook ISBN: 978-1-7332245-3-6

Praise for *Unafraid*

Forbes has listed *Unafraid* as a book that will
help you spark human connections.

"Niyati Tamaskar's story may not be an easy read, but it's a necessary one all the same. After being diagnosed with cancer, Tamaskar was forced to confront the taboo around the disease common in her home country of India. By being honest about her diagnosis and her struggles, Tamaskar broke barriers, hurt feelings, and reformed her relationships in ways she'd never thought possible. *Unafraid* shows the difficulty—and necessity—of connecting with others with a great sense of humor and unforgettable moments of emotion." — *Forbes*

"Niyati Tamaskar boldly tells the story of her cancer journey in unabashed and fearless detail in *Unafraid: A Survivor's Quest for Human Connection*.

"For this active, healthy, happy and high-functioning author, the shock and impact of a breast cancer diagnosis is depicted with intense authenticity, but there is also an impressive matter-of-factness about the prose that doesn't lean heavily on emotional musing. Beautiful moments of reflection are supported by displays of indomitable strength, which make it an essential read for anyone whose life has been touched by cancer.

"Not only is this a viscerally descriptive narrative of a daunting struggle in the author's life, but there are also thought-provoking gems peppered throughout Tamaskar's chronicle. It works both as revealing guide through a traumatic time, as well as an exploration of cultural solidarity and the strength of family." — Editorial Review, SPR

"Little did I know that when I picked up *Unafraid* by Niyati Tamaskar to read, that it would leave such an indelible impression on me. It is by far, the best read of 2019 for me… If you ask me honestly, I'd say that everything in this book works. Mainly because such stories need to be told often, but also because Niyati writes this book from her heart. Raw. Unfiltered. Beautiful.

Unafraid is not just a book; it's a blessing for women out there, and especially to cancer survivors. And we need more such stories." — *Women's Web*, India

DEDICATION

To Nuwan—

Your adventurous spirit gives me wings,
Your fortitude and calm, grounds me.
I love the world we are creating for our children,
With you by my side, I stand tall, *Unafraid.*

CONTENTS

1. INTRODUCTION

**"Learn everything. Fill your mind with knowledge—
it's the only kind of power no one can take
away from you."**
— Min Jin Lee, *Pachinko*

My parents moved from rural India to the metropolis of Bombay after getting married in the late 1970s. Mumbai was still Bombay back then. My father came from a small village in the heart of India called Raigarh, and my mother was from Jabalpur, a town about four hundred miles west. They moved to Bombay with few belongings and a small sum of money and made a life there. This was a bold decision on my father's part; he could have chosen the sheltered life of the village, but he decided to forgo it for bigger and better things. My mother was a doctor. She started a small clinic in the shanties of the city. My father landed a coveted position with American Express as a banker. They came from nothing but worked hard to provide opportunities for my sister and me. My parents faced uncertainty with grit.

Education and moving to a district with better-ranked schools was a top priority for *Baba* (what I call my father in Marathi). *Aai* (mother in Marathi) wanted us to learn the finer things in life such as painting, Indian classical singing, tennis, and swimming. My sister Priyadarshini excelled in sports, at least as much as a girl could in the late '80s and early '90s in India.

She competed in swimming tournaments and was a swim coach in the summer. She was a talented tennis player as well, and even made it to the state championships. I enjoyed singing and was trained in Indian classical music. And I liked to write.

Given all this, the obvious choice for my sister was to get an undergraduate degree in finance and then an MBA, while I worked my way into electrical and computer engineering. Confused? You must not have South Asian parents. Hobbies are great; they make for a good conversation and give you something to hang up in the living room. Sports are a healthy pastime, but they don't pay the bills. Unless they are trust fund babies, the majority of Indian children are molded into doctors, engineers, lawyers, or accountants. Possibly in that order. Allow me to illustrate.

When Priya and I were young girls, Aai enrolled us in swimming lessons. Rain or shine we would go to swim at an outdoor pool called Horizon. Among the kids who came to this pool was a curly-haired young boy who caught my mother's attention. She noticed that he took the city's public transportation to get to the pool, and we would often see him at the bus stop waiting for his ride. At this time it was monsoon season in Mumbai. The scent of earth was intoxicating. When I close my eyes, I can still smell that fragrance, the smell of rain. We could smell it even before it came.

We were pulling out of the parking lot one day when a downpour started, and Aai noticed that young boy at the bus stop. She pulled over to offer him a ride. He gladly took her up on the offer and introduced himself: "*Namaskar*, my name is Sachin." The interrogation started almost immediately: How old are you, What is your favorite subject in school? What are your grades like? What do you want to be when you grow up? You would think Priya and I would be mortified by the cross examination, but we weren't. This was standard practice for all Indian mothers. Sachin was Maharashtrian, like us, so they conversed in Marathi.

Naïvely, Sachin told my mother that he wanted to be a cricketer when he grew up. Priya and I rolled our eyes. How cliché: a young Mumbai city boy dreaming of becoming a cricket star. Aai was kind but firm in her advice: "Sachin, academics should be your top priority. Cricket is a healthy hobby; continue playing sports on the side. But don't neglect your education." Sachin told my mother that he was going to get a chance to play at the national level and that he was a good batsman. There was awkward silence in the car. When we got to Sachin's drop-off point my mother wished him luck. She meant it genuinely. In her eyes, this kid was going to need every last bit of it.

About a year after this incident, Baba was watching a cricket match during dinner when my mother stopped in her tracks. Her jaw dropped. That curly-haired teenager from the pool she had lectured in the car was playing cricket for the Indian national cricket team. His jersey read "Tendulkar"! My mother had told Sachin Tendulkar—who would eventually become a captain of the national team; is regarded as one of the greatest batsmen in the history of cricket; and holds nineteen world records, including the most runs scored by any batsman—that education was more important than pursuing a career in sports. Let that sink in. For those who don't get the irony of this story, here's an analogy that should help: it would be like telling an impressionable young Tom Brady to become an accountant instead of whiling away time playing football. It would be like advising a young Roger Federer to take up a job with the Swiss government, because it's more stable than tennis. This is Indian parenting for you: education above all else. The well-known quote "Failure is not an option" doesn't just apply to NASA. In our home, like so many others, mediocrity is not celebrated, and excellence is expected. It's brutal but simple.

Despite my parents' strong hand, I was blessed to be born into a family of three generations of feminists (four, including me), a lineage of strong, independent, fearless women, and men who supported them. I am now raising my daughter *and son* with the same beliefs, and they will be our family's fifth generation of feminists. It all started with my great-grandparents, who decided to educate my maternal grandmother in the early 1900s in rural India. At the time this was perceived to be unnecessary and futile. Why educate the daughter? The path for women was straightforward: get married, move in with the in-laws, cook, clean, procreate, and raise a family. Education didn't fit this mold. But in their infinite wisdom my great-grandparents sent my *Aaji* (*aaji* is "grandmother" in Marathi) to boarding school as a child and got her educated. My grandmother was married off at the age of eighteen to a humble but immensely progressive young man, my grandfather. He agreed to marry on one condition: that his new bride be allowed to finish university. For a married woman to attend class and finish her education was unheard of in the 1920s, but my Aaji earned her Bachelor of Arts with distinction before having children. The bar was set high, you see.

My grandparents had five girls, and all five were educated. In a society where it is imperative to save money for a dowry, my grandfather decided to invest in his girls' education instead. Education was the dowry, the result of which was three doctors, a PhD dietitian, and a PhD electrical engineer. Did I mention the bar was set high? If I am anything today, it is because of this lineage.

Sometimes I do wonder if subsequent generations accomplish less because they are given more.

• • •

Education had always been the priority. Baba was determined to give us the best possible education, so we moved from the suburbs of Bombay to the heart of the city to go to an all-girls Catholic private school. Catholic schools were touted as having a better educational approach and smaller student-to-teacher ratios, resulting in a classroom environment that was more conducive to learning. There was also an emphasis on English. In India being fluent in English was, and still is, taken as an indicator of how successful you will be. Being a British colony has left its mark, and over time English became the language of the elite in India. Universities, jobs with multinational corporations, and even government jobs require fluency in English. Any hopes of climbing the corporate ladder can be shelved if you can't hold your own in English. Needless to say, a language that has an impact on your socioeconomic status will take center stage in education. So my parents ensured we were fluent in English.

I grew up speaking Marathi, a language spoken by 71 million people in western India and the fourth most-spoken language in the country. My father's side of the family are predominantly speakers of Hindi, the national language of India, and so I also speak Hindi, making me trilingual. Don't be too amazed; this kind of thing is commonplace, and most if not all Indians are multilingual. I was no anomaly.

Any all-girls school has a potent level of toxicity. If you think that kids can be mean, preteen and teenage girls can be vicious. At my school there were cliques of mean girls, pretty girls who were meaner than the mean girls, troublemakers, and teacher's pets. I skirted the line between teacher's pet and troublemaker. It was a tricky business. But my agenda was clear: I wanted to run for student council in tenth grade. (In Bombay, high school is eighth through tenth grades, whereas eleventh and twelfth grades are considered junior college.) You see, leaders in school got to wear a red medal on their school uniforms, distinguishing them from the commoners. This also made the otherwise drab uniform, which consisted of a white blouse paired with a white skirt worn with white socks and black shoes, look special. (Who thinks a white uniform is ideal for prepubescent girls? It made getting our periods an even more dreadful event than it already was.) I shuddered at the thought of spending my senior year of high school in a white uniform with no medal, like a commoner, if I didn't get elected.

I had a plan. I was going to make myself visible. Since I wasn't one of the pretty or popular girls, I put myself on the nerd map by participating in debate competitions and elocutions and by representing my school in interschool competitions. Public speaking, getting up on stage and putting myself out there, was a way to get recognized. It wasn't always a positive experience. There were times when I choked. But I was steadfast and was eventually elected the new Erudite Leader. The word "erudite" means scholarly. How cool is that? I loved that title. Sure, it puts my nerdiness on display, but I was proud of it. I was never going to be one of the popular girls, but I could be a leader of scholars. Better to be Erudite Leader than Sports Leader, in my opinion. As Erudite Leader I organized school debate competitions, trained girls on elocution contests, and held extempore competitions. Senior year of high school was glorious.

I'm a South Bombay girl at heart, and the hard-knock life of the city made me who I am today. Bombay is what gives me an edge over my peers. Street-smart, book-smart, and unafraid is the Bombay mindset. If you weren't one or all three of those things the city would swallow you up whole. We learned that young, and we learned it fast. Competition is fierce from the get-go.

• • •

At the age of eighteen, I moved to the United States to pursue an undergraduate degree in electrical and computer engineering. I was mathematically inclined as a child, geometry was a breeze, and algebra was a fourth language to me. Hence, becoming an engineer was in my destiny. I had gotten accepted into the Ohio State University in Columbus. My mother took a huge leap of faith by letting me pursue this dream of moving to the United States on my own. I had no way of knowing back then that this decision would define the course of my life and, ultimately, give me the resources and strength to face my battle against cancer head-on.

My story is a culmination of epic fumbles, brilliant coincidences, extraordinary twists of fate, and divine intervention. It is the story of an immigrant, an engineer, a wife, and a mother. But more importantly, it is the story of a cancer survivor.

2. THE DIAGNOSIS

"I feel like the word *shatter*."
— Margaret Atwood, *The Handmaid's Tale*

It was a Sunday night when I noticed a lump in my left breast. It felt like a plugged milk duct of sorts, a medium-sized mass that was squishy and moveable. I was breastfeeding and figured it might be the start of mastitis. I spent most of Monday draining the breast and making sure my one-year-old daughter, Aarini, drank from the left side. But the lump persisted, and I told my husband, Nuwan, about it. He said I should call my OB, our neighbor and dear friend Degaulle. On Tuesday morning I called his office; they said they wanted to see me right away. I really didn't think it was that urgent, but I was not about to ignore my symptoms and let this manifest into a full-blown mastitis attack. Nuwan came to the appointment with me, as he always does. I can count on one hand the number of doctor's appointments he has missed, and this is after two pregnancies. He is always by my side.

Nuwan and I were then living in Columbus, Indiana, where we still live. Not to be confused with the lesser-known Columbus, Ohio, where I went to school for my undergraduate degree, this Columbus is the location of my obstetrician's office, who confirmed both my pregnancies, and of the hospital where I delivered my babies; and so it holds a special place in my heart.

The nurse practitioner at Degaulle's office did a swift breast exam and told me that it wasn't one lump, but two. They were very indicative of cysts, she said: squishy, moveable, almost swollen. She added that most cancers are pea-sized and rigid. She put our worries to rest but still scheduled me for an ultrasound and mammogram. I was really annoyed about being forced to get a mammogram, my first ever. I told her I had dense, breastfeeding, milk-filled breasts. The mammogram was not only going to be uncomfortable, it could potentially flag false positives. I was sure of it. But the office simply said that with a family history of breast cancer—my mother had it at age forty-four—I was a prime candidate for an early mammogram. I was told that the general guidelines for getting mammograms are to take the age when your blood relative was diagnosed with cancer and subtract ten years. Annoyingly, I was thirty-four, so the math worked out perfectly.

The mammogram was not as painful as I had imagined. My stomach wasn't in knots; I just wanted to get it over with. After the scan, the ultrasound technician took me in. She did some quick measurements of my cyst and asked me to return to the waiting room. Nuwan was asked to wait at the reception area. After I was done, the nurse brought him back into the waiting room with me. We made small talk as we waited for the radiologist. Dr. Matthews called us into a dark room, where the images of my mammogram were displayed on a computer screen. As he started to talk about the cysts I felt my body go numb. He said that this could be an infection, or it could be cancer. The odds were 50-50, and so he couldn't say if the chances were weighted one way or the other.

Nuwan and I couldn't believe it. There was NO WAY this was cancer. I felt like I was in the prime of my health: I was back to my pre-pregnancy weight, and I was enjoying breastfeeding and being a mother of two.

I was working full-time. There was no indication that I might be sick. Dr. Matthews showed us the inflamed, enlarged lymph nodes indicating that my body was fighting an infection—or something worse. I was done hearing the word "cancer". I asked for next steps. "How do we confirm this *isn't* cancer?" Dr. Matthews recommended a biopsy and gave me two options: fitting us in the same day or scheduling it a week later. I remember begging him at this point; I wanted the biopsy right away. He cautioned us that, even after the biopsy, it could take up to a week for the results if additional analysis was required. But I was convinced that it wasn't cancer, and we just needed the doctors to confirm that. Dr. Matthews obligingly scheduled the biopsy for me the same day.

Nuwan wasn't allowed to be in the room with me during the process. I started to feel lonely and nervous. Why couldn't he be by my side? He's always by my side. He was there for the birth of both our children, in the delivery room; he cut the umbilical cord, he held my hand, and he rubbed my back during contractions . . . he is always by my side. He waited in a private waiting room while I was taken into a sterile exam room for a vacuum-assisted core biopsy. Three sites were biopsied: the two lumps and one lymph node. Dr. Matthews injected the site with local anesthetic and then started the procedure. The anesthetic didn't work. I could feel pain, I told Dr. Matthews, and he immediately injected me with more anesthetic and continued. I could sense blood trickling down my sides, and I started to cry. The ultrasound technician held my hand and told me I was doing so well. She was an angel, the sweetest person with the kindest eyes. She told me to keep breathing.

The biopsy was a horrid experience. It wasn't that Dr. Matthews was unkind. In fact, the whole team was empathetic. They encouraged me, told me I was doing so great. But the experience itself was traumatizing. I told them I regretted reporting the lumps, regretted this whole episode. If I had just kept the information to myself, I thought, I would've been fine. During the biopsy I kept thinking about Nuwan. What did I drag him into? He must have been scared and nervous too, for me. *It cannot be cancer; obviously, it's not cancer.* But what a nauseating way to confirm that. I told the ultrasound technician to go to the waiting room and tell Nuwan that I was okay. "Please make sure he hasn't passed out," I joked.

Dr. Matthews had told me that during the biopsy he was going to insert a titanium marker into the mass. This marker would show up in subsequent mammograms to indicate the site has been biopsied. I asked him about the size of this marker. He said it was less than 2 millimeters. He assured me it wouldn't trigger any airport metal detectors and, because it wasn't a ferrous material, was completely safe. *Boobs of titanium,* I thought to myself. *I'm practically Iron Woman. I have superpowers.* My mind has this amazing ability to find humor and courage in the toughest of situations. It is a coping mechanism and a survival tool for me. *I am Iron Woman. I got this. I'm a South Bombay girl. I spent my whole childhood learning to handle tough situations.*

My left breast was bruised and sore. The team of doctors now wanted another mammogram, but I was ready for this nightmare to be over. My legs felt numb, and my knees were weak. I couldn't stand for the next mammogram. They made me sit for it and adjusted the height of the machine. I felt sick. What a demoralizing experience. I told myself I was never going to report a lump again. By the time the nurses took me back to Nuwan, I was done crying. I just said to him, "Honey, I wish they had let you come in so you could be with me. I wish you were with me." We sat down for a bit. I had some oranges and fruit which I'd brought in my purse. I ate to raise my blood sugar levels. I felt better, and we drove home. The nightmare was finally over. I decided I would never put myself and Nuwan through this experience again.

I had requested that the radiologist give me a copy of his report and the scans. They couldn't provide scans to me on the spot, but they were happy to give me a copy of the doctor's dictation. The report was thorough. It had a lot of alarming words in there, phrases that I didn't Google. What if Dr. Google confirmed my worst nightmares? I told myself it was better to wait for the Breast Health Center to call back and confirm that it wasn't cancer. I had decided it wouldn't be cancer. But I was afraid, and I reached out to my cousin, an internist and the most brilliant doctor I know, Vikram *dada* (a Marathi term of reverence used when addressing an older brother). I narrated my experience to him and read the notes from the report. He reassured me it could not be cancer. It just wasn't feasible; I was thirty-four and breastfeeding.

Vikram is a master of analogies. He can explain the most complex medical phenomena with the most basic, understandable illustration. Our talk was no exception. He explained that normal cells are like an engine. (His analogies are always engine- or automobile-related when he talks to Nuwan and me.) If a normal cell is operating at 2,000 RPM, a cancer cell operates at an extremely elevated level—say, 30,000 RPM. As a breastfeeding mother, he said, my mammary glands were overworked. These cells were probably operating at 8,000 RPM and flagged a concern that the doctors noticed. But they were nowhere close to cancer cell-level speed, said Vikram. The radiologist saw anomalies in the cells, but it wasn't because of cancer. I reiterated how I regretted reporting the lump. He laughed and assured me that I did the right thing, and that the radiologist did the right thing too. Everyone was operating within the confines of what was medically advised. I asked him point blank, "Dada, if you were the radiologist, and you knew the patient was a breastfeeding mother, would you have put her through this ordeal?" I could hear him shuffling his feet a bit, not coming clean with me. I pressed him for an answer. He finally said, "Yes. In my medical opinion I would have done the same thing. But Niyati, this is not cancer."

On Friday, March 2, 2018, I woke up wondering when this nightmare would be over. My left breast was bruised and yellowish green. The biopsy sites were sore. I felt miserable. I breastfed Aarini on my right breast, and Nuwan dropped the kids off at daycare. We stayed home for a couple hours that morning, since I felt like I needed to rest. Nuwan worked on his slides on corporate strategy; he had a presentation at 11:00 a.m. We sat waiting for the call that would confirm this wasn't cancer. Nuwan left home at 10:30 a.m. to make his meeting, and I then turned on the television to distract myself. The doctor's office still hadn't called.

At 11:10 a.m. I decided to call the Breast Health Center myself. Vikram had warned me not to be too eager, explaining that sometimes they need to send the sample in for additional dye testing, which can take up to a week. I needed this nightmare to be over, so I called anyway. A nurse picked up the phone. "Your results just came in. All three sites tested positive for cancer."

My heart sank, and my body went numb. The nightmare became reality. She told me I had Grade 3 invasive ductile carcinoma. The grading is an indication of how aggressive the cancer is; tumors are graded between 1 (low) and 3 (high).

This cannot be happening. I am thirty-four years old and breastfeeding. Wasn't breastfeeding supposed to reduce the risk of getting breast cancer? That's what I had been told. My daughter had just turned one. My son Vihaan was only three and a half years old. And I had Nuwan. *This cannot be happening.*

I paced up and down for a few seconds, my mind racing. I needed to tell Nuwan. Do I call him? Do I tell him in person? Should I drive to his office? I called Vikram instead. He didn't answer the phone. *Somebody just tell me what to do! How do I tell Nuwan?*

I called Nuwan. "Honey, are you in your meeting?"

He said yes, but that he had stepped out.

"Darling, it's cancer. I have cancer. Come home, I need you."

Nuwan choked up. "I'm coming home, I'm coming to you." He ran out of his meeting, tears streaming down his face, and drove home.

I knew I had to tell my sister and my mother in India right away. I called my sister. "Priya, can you hear me? Is the baby okay? What are you doing right now?"

Priya had had a baby girl four months earlier. Nuwan and I had booked tickets for the four of us to visit my family in India, Nuwan's sister Priyanka and her family in Dubai, and Nuwan's parents in Sri Lanka. We were supposed to leave in two weeks. It was going to be a big family holiday.

"Priya, I have breast cancer. Grade 3 invasive ductile breast cancer."

She started screaming and crying and shouting. I could hear my brother-in-law, Kamlesh, in the background asking her, "What happened? What's wrong, Priya?" I told her I had to hang up, that our mother deserved to hear the news right away, and that I wanted to call her. Priya said she was going over to Aai's place right away; they both live in the same apartment complex. I called my mother several times, but she didn't answer the phone. Nuwan was still on his way home from work. Time seemed to be moving so slowly.

My mother finally answered the phone. "Aai, can you hear me?"

"Yes, I'm just getting ready for bed. What's going on?"

"Aai, I have breast cancer."

The rest of my conversation with my mother is a blur. Priya and Kamlesh got to Aai's place to comfort her. I hung up the phone and called Vikram, but it went to voicemail. I did not have the words to leave a message.

I sat on the couch, slumped, waiting for my husband. Nuwan walked through the door. He looked at me, dropped to his knees, and started to cry. I cried.

"I have cancer, honey. What are we going to do?"

We cried some more. I have two children, a husband and cancer.

Vikram called back. "Niyati, sorry. I was in the shower—you called?"

"Dada, I have cancer."

"What do you mean you have cancer?"

"The biopsy confirmed cancer in three sites: the two lumps and the lymph node. They are calling it Grade 3 invasive ductile breast cancer."

Silence.

That afternoon Vikram and his wife Beena packed their bags and drove two hundred miles from Ohio to Columbus to be with us.

Nuwan and I couldn't sleep that night. We just lay there awake in bed, shell-shocked. I was still breastfeeding, and my daughter co-slept with us. Oblivious to the cancer, all she wanted was her mother and breastmilk. She used my nipple like a pacifier. The night was quiet; I could hear Aarini suckling and feel my heart thumping. How could this be happening to us? And how were we going to get through it?

3. MY BETTER HALF

**"I asked you here tonight because when you realize
you want to spend the rest of your life with somebody,
you want the rest of your life to start as
soon as possible."**
— Graeme Simsion, *The Rosie Project*

In 2005, upon graduating, I moved from Ohio to Peoria, Illinois to work for a Fortune 500 company, which was sponsoring my H-1B work visa. Life as an immigrant made me all too familiar with the visa process. I had gone from having an F-1 student visa, during my undergrad years, to enrolling in a temporary work program called Optional Practical Training, and then to obtaining an H-1B.

With work came financial freedom, and with financial freedom came the chance to travel! On my bucket list were traveling to Peru and hiking to Machu Picchu. In the spring of 2008, I started planning this dream vacation with friends. It was going to be my first time in South America and the Southern Hemisphere. The four-day hike from the city of Cusco to Machu Picchu is a tough twenty-six miles of mainly climbing steps. The altitude doesn't help. You start at 10,000 feet above sea level and go up to almost 14,000 feet on the second day, only to end at just 8,000 feet above sea level.

I started training hard for this trip six months in advance. I was the ringleader for the adventure, organizing friends from Japan, South Korea, Wisconsin, Illinois, and Canada. I ran into some issues with hotel bookings and realized I needed help from a Spanish-speaking compadre. I went to none other than my totally crazy Mexican American friend Miguel, who used his charm and Spanish-language skills to sort out the bookings for me. I asked Miguel if he knew anyone who had done the four-day hike, because I was a bit anxious and wanted to talk to someone who had. He said he knew just the man for the job, a British Sri Lankan friend of his named Nuwan Gallege. Miguel set up an evening for us to meet at Jimmy's, a local Irish pub in Peoria. Miguel was there too, and he introduced me to Nuwan.

Nuwan was a handsome, six-foot-tall, British-sounding, Sri Lankan-looking hunk of a man. *Now that's a tall drink of water,* I thought to myself. (Don't worry—this isn't going to turn into a romance novel. Sheesh!) What captivated me about Nuwan was his passion for travel, which far surpassed mine. In fact, Nuwan and Miguel were planning a trip to Argentina, to explore Patagonia, during the time I was going to be in Peru hiking. Nuwan and I chatted about what to expect on the hike, the temperature swings, and some things to watch out for. He told me altitude sickness is one of the biggest issues. We chatted away the evening, and when it was over I didn't know where the time had gone.

A month after our trips, Miguel had a farewell party, as he was moving from Peoria to Baltimore. The turnout for the party was impressive; never before had I seen so many international people gathered under one roof. Brazilians, Mexicans, Indians, Americans, Brits, Colombians—many ethnicities and languages were represented. Spanish, Portuguese, Hindi, and English words filled the air. I was a wallflower that day, because I didn't know anyone at the party. That is, till Nuwan walked in. I was happy to see a familiar face in the crowd. We migrated towards each other to share recent holiday stories. I was over the moon about conquering "Dead Woman's Pass", the highest point of the Machu Picchu hike at 13,829 feet.

Nuwan told me about his and Miguel's adventures in Patagonia. He also talked about his upcoming trip to Thailand and Cambodia. I mentioned my plans to go to Spain and Portugal over Christmas, and he recommended some unique places to check out in Spain, such as Ronda and Grenada. I was awestruck by his passion for travel. Clearly something about me interested him, too, because it wasn't long before he asked me out on a date. Score!

Nuwan came to pick me up for our first date in a black convertible BMW Z4. It was crisp fall evening on October 8, 2008. We ate dinner at the Rhythm Kitchen in Peoria, one of my favorite restaurants. The conversation was endless; there was an instant spark between us. Dating Nuwan was effortless. There was no drama or games, just raw honesty. Of course, like any new couple, we put our best foot forward at the beginning, but we never shied away from saying what was on our minds.

Nuwan was born in South Kensington, London to a Sri Lankan Buddhist family. His family moved to Sri Lanka when he was five years old. When he returned to the motherland, he attended a Sinhalese school. Nuwan talked about the challenges he faced as a five-year-old transitioning from a British (English) school to an all-Sinhalese one. He spoke about the civil war in Sri Lanka and how that affected his schooling. Public schools were shut down for extended lengths of time. Government-mandated curfews affected day-to-day living, not to mention the impact suicide bombings, air raids, and military actions had on a young mind. Eventually Nuwan's parents moved him and his sister Priyanka into private school in order to continue their education uninterrupted.

Nuwan moved back to England when he turned eighteen, to attend the University of Surrey for his bachelor's in mechanical engineering. After graduating he started working for Dozer Co. in Leicester. A few years into his career he got an opportunity to move to the US on an expatriate assignment. These are highly coveted postings; only the brightest engineers get asked to move internationally.

Our relationship became more official the day Nuwan told his landlords, Grant and Bobbie, about me. They were like family to him, so this sort of disclosure was not out of the ordinary. Bobbie's description of that day never fails to amuse me. Apparently, when Nuwan had come over to pay his rent, he stepped out of his shiny BMW with a great big smile on his face. Bobbie immediately knew something was up. Nuwan said to her, "Bobbie, I've met a girl!" Bobbie's face lights up like the fourth of July whenever she narrates this story. She had been pining to hear those words from Nuwan for a long time. In fact, I'm pretty sure Bobbie was already planning our wedding when she heard this. Grant was pleased too, and they wanted to meet me. It was an honor to meet Grant and Bobbie after all the stories Nuwan had told me about them. They were like parents to him, and he was as close as a son to them.

• • •

On our eight-month anniversary, in June 2009, Nuwan planned a surprise for me. It was a Friday, and I had had a blah day at work, firefighting multiple engineering issues. I came back exhausted and ready for the weekend. When I went to my bedroom, there was a long-stemmed red rose on my bed with a card. I opened the envelope to find it wasn't a card, actually—it was a clue as to the whereabouts of the next rose hidden somewhere in the house. Nuwan had planned an entire scavenger hunt using our dating history as clues: the first movie we watched together, the green jacket I wore on our hiking trip to Starved Rock State Park, and more. It was endearing to find roses all over the house. The last clue informed me that we were going to the "best restaurant in town." There was a French bistro I liked, and I figured Nuwan was going to take me there. I wore an elegant black dress and texted him. I couldn't wait to see him.

Nuwan asked me to drive to "707 W. Versailles Drive" for my last and final clue. The address was Nuwan's place. I tried not to speed as I drove to his house. The final clue read, "Follow the candlelight trail to the back of the house." There were candles everywhere; it was so romantic. I made my way to the back of the house, and my jaw dropped. Nuwan had set up a candlelight dinner for us in his back yard. There was a beautiful table with a crisp white tablecloth, new plates, elegant silverware, and champagne chilling next to some champagne flutes—the works! I finally got it: the best restaurant in town was Nuwan's backyard, with Chef Nuwan cooking up a decadent meal. It was so romantic. He had put in so much effort to make this evening special.

He served up a four-course meal. It was perfect. When it was time for dessert, he asked me to close my eyes and make a wish. I opened my eyes, and Nuwan was down on one knee with a ring in his hand. He proposed to me with the most stunning diamond ring I had ever seen—oh, the sparkle!

He asked, "Will you marry me?"

I said, "Yes!"

We had two weddings, because why have one destination wedding when you can have two? We had a Hindu ceremony in Mumbai, followed by a Buddhist ceremony in Sri Lanka in December 2009. We invited several friends, hoping one or two would be lured by the prospect of travel and adventure, but the response we got was overwhelming. We were overjoyed, but knew we needed to educate our potential guests about traveling to South Asia. Nuwan built a website with information about the Hindu wedding, travel to India, guidance on completing the visa application, and options for hotels. He had another page dedicated to the Buddhist ceremony and Sri Lanka. There was no dissuading the nerd herd now.

We had friends from the US, England, and Australia flying across the world to be part of our special days. To add to that mix, I had Russian friends who planned to fly in from St. Petersburg: Kostya, my brother from another mother, and his stunning wife Nastya. This one's for you, brother—*Hindi Russi bhai bhai.*

My relatives flew from the US to be there for our big day. Uncles, aunts, cousins, and their spouses flew from New York, Washington D.C., Boston, Cleveland, Chicago, and Seattle. I am certain my wedding single-handedly boosted the Indian tourism market with all the international folks attending.

The Indian wedding was my version of *My Big Fat Greek Wedding*, only bigger and crazier (and with less spanakopita). It was a three-day extravaganza, pulled together by Aai, Priya, and Kamlesh. I took over the reins of organizing airport pickups, hotel bookings, and shopping trips. My mother had living arrangements made for all the relatives attending the wedding. At Indian weddings the host pays for your living arrangements and meals for the duration of the wedding. In the US, paying for everyone's hotel bills would be considered preposterous, but that's how it's done at home. Aai even hired a chef and a small army of helpers to serve fresh meals and hot chai to the guests—for all three days!

Our foreign guests all wanted to wear Indian clothes for the wedding, which delighted me. Sarees, salwars, kurtas—the bright and bedazzling colors of Indian attire is hard to top. It was a visual treat.

The first day of the wedding was the henna ceremony. My hands and feet were adorned with henna in intricate patterns. We had extra artists around to put henna on any of the women who wanted it. My mother had hired *bhangra* dancers to entertain the crowds. (Bhangra is a dance style of the Sikh people from Northern India.) These men came with their own *dhol* (Indian drums). They sang folk songs in Punjabi, performed dazzling acrobatics, and got the crowd on their feet. It was a great start to the wedding. I met some of Nuwan's closest friends for the first time: two chaps from England, a fellow from North Carolina, and a Southern gentleman from Georgia. Aunty Jensine and Uncle Colin came from Australia, possibly the farthest anyone had traveled. I enjoyed socializing with everyone and getting to know Nuwan's inner circle.

On the second day we had a pre-wedding reception called the *sangeet*. The *sangeet* is traditionally a time for the two families to get acquainted with each other. It's also a time for the bride and groom to talk to each other; given that most marriages in India are arranged, they may not have had many opportunities yet. My cousins and friends put together skits, songs, and dances to entertain the guests. A few of my mother's colleagues gave speeches, and my uncle, a radiologist, did a stand-up comedy routine. Nuwan's childhood friend Kalinga gave a hilarious speech that started with, "Hi, I'm Kalinga, and unlike everyone else before me, I am not a doctor." Everyone was in splits during his speech. I especially loved the bit where he said something about how, "Nuwan moved to the US, bought the fastest car, and married the prettiest girl." The highlight of the *sangeet* was a choreographed dance performance by my sister and brother-in-law. The amount of practice they had put in was made more than apparent by their fluid movements and flawless execution.

On December 21, 2009—winter solstice, the shortest day of the year— Nuwan and I got married in a traditional Hindu wedding. In Hindu weddings, the bride is at the altar while the groom comes in on a white horse (technically, a mare). As the groom rides in like a knight in shining armor, the groom's family takes to the city streets and dances. This procession is called the *baraat*. Picture this: Nuwan on a white horse in the busy streets of Mumbai. A quartet of drummers and trumpeters drowning out the noise of the traffic with music. Friends and family—Indians, Sri Lankans, Americans, Brits, and even some Russians—dancing in the street as the groom makes his way to the wedding venue on a white mare. It was spectacular.

• • •

Afew days after the wedding we flew to Sri Lanka for the Buddhist ceremony. The Hindu wedding was Nuwan's first visit to India, and the Buddhist one was my first visit to Sri Lanka.

The Buddhist ceremony was unique, at least in my eyes. The priest tied our index fingers together, hence "tying the knot". (I wonder if this is the origin of the phrase.) After the Buddhist wedding Nuwan organized a small tour of Sri Lanka for us. You're thinking honeymoon, right? Wrong. By "us" I mean that Nuwan invited thirty-four of our friends and members of our immediate family on a four-day tour of his motherland. It was a memorable trip that left a lasting impact on all of us. So much so that, six months later, a fellow engineer came up to Nuwan one day saying, "Hey, you had that big wedding in India and Sri Lanka, right?" Nuwan, perplexed said, "Yes?" The engineer told him one of the guests from our wedding had given a presentation about his experience in India and Sri Lanka in a team meeting. We were famous.

Soon after we got married, Nuwan was given an opportunity to go back to the UK. Alternatively, he could continue to stay in the US and get his permanent residency here. We decided to embrace the adventure of living in England. A lot of people told us we were making a mistake, that we should stay, start the green card process, obtain US permanent residency, and then move to the UK at some future time. We looked at it the opposite way: an opportunity to relocate to the UK with a US-based company doesn't come around often. The path back to the mothership was something we could figure out if we wanted to do so in the future. It might sound arrogant coming from a twenty-six-year-old, but I really didn't feel like the doors of America would be closed to us if we moved to the UK without our green cards. I had a powerful network. If I were to find a position back in the US, we could always relocate on a work visa, such as H-1B or L-1, and then apply for permanent residency. And I was just plain excited about the prospect of living in Europe! The biggest draw for me was the merely eight-hour nonstop flight from London to Mumbai, which would cut my travel time by more than half. I could go home at the drop of a hat, relatively speaking.

My job situation was going to be a challenge with the international move. Nuwan and I both worked for Dozer Co. While he had an excellent opportunity waiting for him in England, the role I was getting was far from ideal. I felt like I was the second part of a "buy one, get one free" deal. So I decided to interview and find a job elsewhere. I was fortunate to land a really exciting engine electronics and controls position with Engine Co. in Daventry, England. So I accepted that offer and resigned from Dozer Co., and we moved to England.

As foolish as it might have seemed, this move was a bold one. It takes courage to move internationally, even from one English-speaking country to another. It would test our marriage and communication skills: how we handled stressful situations, worked through challenges, and continued to thrive as a couple. We had made similar moves in the past when we were younger and more unprepared. Nuwan moved from Sri Lanka to the UK when he was eighteen, and I moved from India to the US when I was the same age. We were ready for this new adventure—an opportunity that would come to shape my career and help me to grow as a person.

• • •

The next big step of our marriage and adulthood was . . . no, not kids! I was in no rush to have babies. I loved the freedom that came with having a dual income and no kids. To be able to say, on a Friday, "Let's take the Mini on a ferry across the channel, land in Dunkirk, and then drive from France to Bruges," because we felt like it was marvelous. I was in no hurry to give that up.

The next step of adulthood came when we bought a townhouse in the town of Royal Leamington Spa. (Side note: I love how the English use "royal" and "great" in their town names.) Leamington is considered posh, with beautiful gardens, water fountains, and an old Victorian bathhouse at the center. Our house was in the city center, and within walking distance to the greengrocer, fishmonger, and local shopping center. When we walked into the place for our first viewing, the surprisingly low price of the house started to make sense. The owners were smokers, so it reeked of the stench of smoke. Several walls had wallpaper on them. The ceiling was wallpapered too. Who puts wallpaper on the ceiling? Nuwan and I wanted to renovate the house while preserving and enhancing its original features. We wanted a fixer-upper. So we made an offer, and in October 2012, Nuwan and I became homeowners.

The renovation process tested our relationship. The late nights of physical labor on top of long days at work were challenging, but they honed our communication and decision-making skills. We made a good team. I feel these big, challenging experiences before my cancer diagnosis helped strengthen our bond and prepare us for the journey ahead. International moves are tough, and going through immigration processes and all the paperwork involved with relocation can be daunting. But we got through that. And now, on the other side of the pond, we had bought and renovated a house. Every step was character-building.

Nuwan and I hosted many family gatherings and events in that home. On cold and dreary winter evenings when we didn't have visitors, we would relax in the living room, drink fine English ales, listen to the crackles of the wood-burning fireplace, and play records. I long for those days. I didn't know it then, but life was so simple, untarnished by cancer.

While living in the UK, Nuwan and I worked for rival engineering companies. I worked at Engine Co., and Nuwan worked at Dozer Co. We didn't talk about work at home. His forte and engineering experience was in powertrain design (transmission and torque converters—nerd alert!). My career had started taking shape in the engine world. I worked on 60- and 91-liter natural gas engines that are used for power generation. We wondered how long this could last, us working for rival companies, as we both started to climb the corporate ladder.

One afternoon at Engine Co. we had a vice president onsite. Matt had traveled from the US to England for a quarterly update. Profit, earnings, ROI, warranty dollars . . . yawn. I zoned in and out of the presentation, lost in thought about an engine controls issue that I needed to fix. Priorities, people!

I snapped out of my daze when Matt said the word "powertrain." I tuned in and learned that Engine Co. was making a huge investment in this area. This would expand the portfolio of our Fortune 500 company immensely and was a huge step towards vertical integration. My ears perked up, and I was intrigued; would this be an opportunity for Nuwan to jump ship and start working at Engine Co.? The answer became obvious when Matt ended that segment with, "If you know any engineers with powertrain experience . . ." This was it—I had to make a move.

I emailed Matt's administrative assistant after the meeting asking for fifteen minutes of his time. She promptly wrote back saying he was busy, and his calendar was fully booked. I thought for a few minutes and decided, *To heck with it, I'll email Matt directly. What's the worst that could happen?*

The subject line of my email read "Dozer Co. Engineer with 12 years of Powertrain Experience." That got his attention, all right. Matt's administrative assistant called me directly on my desk phone ten minutes later and asked if I was free to meet with Matt at 6:45 p.m. Of course I was free. For the next step I needed Nuwan's resume, something he hadn't updated in years. I called Nuwan and asked him to dust off the old document, spiff it up, and email it to me. With his swiftly updated resume in hand, I was ready for my meeting with Matt. Nuwan's oil and gas experience, work in the field, and extensive knowledge of powertrain design impressed Matt, and before long HR sent Nuwan an interview date.

Nuwan aced the interviews: one over the phone, one over Skype, and then a face-to-face meeting with several managers in Columbus, Indiana, where the company's corporate headquarters were located. Nuwan landed the job. But it was in the United States, which meant we would have to pack up shop and move across the pond—again! We had bought and renovated this beautiful home, and had just started to get to know our neighbors and establish roots in the UK. I thought maybe England was where we would start a family, given the generous maternity leave that Britons get, with twenty-six weeks of full pay. But this was a huge opportunity for Nuwan, and we decided to seize it.

When we got back to the US I hit the ground running. I knew most of my colleagues since I had collaborated closely with the US team while based in England. I had also come to the US on work trips and so had established some connections. Nuwan and I started making new friends at work. We moved into a beautiful rental property on the north side of town with a three-car garage, cathedral ceilings, and a massive kitchen. Welcome to the American dream.

There was one thing about Columbus that I didn't know before we moved there. The town did not offer recycling services! That frustrated me to no end. To throw away cans, bottles, and recyclable plastic made no sense to me. In England recycling is encouraged. It's the norm. In fact in London, you can get fined for throwing recyclables into regular trash. One evening I saw a green recycling bin outside my neighbor's house. I said to Nuwan, "I wonder what recycling service they use. This isn't processed through the city." I asked him if I should go over to the neighbor's house and inquire. He vehemently said no. I figured that, clearly, these people thought like us and valued recycling, and that I should go introduce myself.

Against my British husband's reclusive nature, I knocked on the neighbor's door. A sweet lady opened it and invited me in without hesitation. We hit it off, and she told me she was from D.C. and had three girls. Her name was Ghalila. She gave me details of the recycling pickup service she used, and we exchanged phone numbers. Since we were new to town, she told me to contact her if we needed anything at all. I loved being back in the Midwest! People here are inherently kind. I don't know if this is a stereotype, or if I had blinders on before. But I promise you, there's no place like the Midwest.

The first winter we were in Columbus, there was a massive snowstorm. All we had was a snow shovel, and Nuwan was out in the driveway trying to beat back the eight to ten inches of snow on the ground. I was out with him but of no help. In Nuwan's words, I have the upper-body strength of linguine. He had only finished shoveling part of the driveway by the time we went to sleep. The next morning, it snowed again. We made it to work okay, but with the new snowfall, he was going to need to clear the driveway again. When we got home, though, to our surprise, the driveway had been shoveled! Almost professionally, in fact, with the edges shaped neatly. I looked over at Ghalila's driveway, and hers looked the same. I assumed it was the handiwork of Ghalila's husband, whom we hadn't met yet. When I texted to thank her, she told me it was another neighbor down the street named Karl who had done our driveways. He didn't even know us, and he shoveled our driveway in the middle of a storm. Do you still question my claim about midwestern values?! People here are something else. Let's just say it was good to be back.

● ● ●

I reflect on our move back to the US often. It was a fortunate stroke of serendipity to end up in a country that boasts of the top ten cancer hospitals in the world. Cancer treatment in the United States is unparalleled. The American Cancer Society also standardizes this treatment, which means that a patient from a rural area will receive the same treatment and class of drugs as a patient in the big city. This isn't the case in other parts of the world. I feel fortunate that I was at work the day the vice president visited my UK office. I like to call it the work of destiny, which by the way, is the meaning of my name! *Niyati* means "destiny" in Sanskrit, an ancient Indo-European language that originated in India.

4. PARENTHOOD

"For you, a thousand times over."
— Khaled Hosseini, *The Kite Runner*

January 1, 2014 seemed like an auspicious day to pee on a stick. I had sneaked out to the pharmacy the night before to pick up a home-pregnancy test. The two-minute wait for the result seemed like an eternity. I left the test on the bathroom sink and proceeded to brush my teeth a second time, just to distract myself. A few seconds later I looked at the test and did a double take: there was a "Yes+" in the display window. It said, "Yes+". I was pregnant! *Can women get pregnant this fast?* I ran to Nuwan and screamed, "Honey!" He looked at me strangely, perplexed at the sight of the pregnancy test in my hand. "I'm pregnant!" I blurted out. He was ecstatic; he kissed me and then looked at the test to make sure it confirmed my announcement. I said to him, "It's positive. We are going to have a baby!" I was five weeks pregnant. And just like that we started a new phase of our life.

Within minutes of knowing that we were expecting, I downloaded two pregnancy apps and entered in all my data. The due date was predicted to be August 31: Labor Day weekend. I chuckled at the irony of going into labor on Labor Day.

Our first doctor's visit was with a nurse, a sort of sanity check to confirm the pregnancy, followed by my first prenatal exam to check the fetus's health. Nuwan and I went into a dark room, and a friendly ultrasound technician named Carla came in to perform our first ultrasound. She squirted cold gel on my belly and pressed the ultrasound probe hard against my stomach. In less than a second the screen showed my uterus and a little peanut inside it. The peanut, though, had a head and a body. I was in love. I was in awe.

Carla swiftly took some fetal measurements and then turned on the sound. PA-POW, PA-POW, PA-POW—we could hear the baby's heartbeat. Peanut's heart was thrumming at 167 beats per minute. It was the most beautiful sound I had ever heard. Inside my body there was a little fetus, 1.75 centimeters long, a coffee bean with a human head and a strong, pounding heart. I turned my head to the right to look at the screen and, in that moment of elation, a sneaky little tear escaped my eyes. Before we were done, I asked Carla if we could hear the heartbeat again. She obliged. PA-POW, PA-POW, PA-POW, PA-POW. I could've listened to that all day. I asked her if could get some pictures. She obliged again. There, on glossy paper, was evidence—evidence that Nuwan and I had created a life, and that my body was a safe home in which it could grow.

We've sent a man to the moon and mapped the human genome. We have advanced technology at our fingertips and in our pockets. Yet this antiquated ultrasound machine with its rudimentary capabilities gave me the greatest joy: the sound of my child's heartbeat. What a miracle!

• • •

When it came to finding a doctor, Nuwan and I imagined that things would be like they are in the movies: we would interview several obstetricians in town during the early stages of the pregnancy, then, after careful evaluation, would pick the one we liked the most. The OB/GYN would be at our beck and call, answering frantic midnight questions and responding to my texts. And then, when the time came, she would rush to the hospital to deliver our child. Yes, my obstetrician was going to be a woman.

Reality was a pole apart from our rom-com fantasy. There is only one hospital in Columbus, and, when I was pregnant, six obstetricians practiced there—and only one female OB. You could interview them all and see whomever you'd like, but at the end of the day, the obstetrician who was on-call when you went into labor would be the one delivering the baby. That was a bit disappointing.

Determined to not let this get to me, I decided to rotate and see all the obstetricians, just so a familiar face would deliver our child. I started with the only female obstetrician in town. She was lovely! I liked her instantly… till she said, "I'm sure you've noticed I'm twenty-eight weeks pregnant. It'll be time for me to have a baby soon." Did you hear something shatter? Those were my dreams. There was no way she would be back from maternity leave in time to deliver my spawn. Next!

The second obstetrician we saw was a jerk who shall remain unnamed. He was unkind and egotistical. Let me explain. It all began during my twelve-week appointment. As you may know, the twelfth week marks the end of the first trimester, the period during which most miscarriages occur. As a result, most women like to keep their pregnancy hidden until the first trimester is over. It had been a precarious three months, and Nuwan and I were hopeful that, after this appointment, we could share the good news with our friends and family. Something strange, though, had seemed to happen right at the twelve-week mark, and I was anxious to ask the doctor about it. I had suddenly stopped feeling all the symptoms of the pregnancy. I wasn't fatigued or nauseous anymore.

When the doctor came to the room, he went straight to check the fetal heartrate with his hand-held doppler device. "I've stopped feeling symptoms," I said, but he had no time for my concerns. I could hear the heartbeat on his device, which brought a smile to my face. "That's not the baby—that's your heartbeat," he said as he pressed the probe a bit harder on my belly to find the fetal heartbeat. At this point my own heartrate started to skyrocket, and we could hear it. He muttered under his breath, "Come on, come on." I started to cry. Nuwan held my hand; he was worried, too, but wanted to comfort me.

A minute later the doctor gave up. He said we needed to get an ultrasound to confirm if the fetus was still alive. Then he looked at my chart and said, "It is not uncommon for women over thirty to have a miscarriage in the first trimester." This doctor couldn't find a heartbeat with this archaic handheld device, so he declared my geriatric, over-thirty status the culprit and the potential reason for a miscarriage. I was inconsolable, but demanded that we get an ultrasound immediately. "It's not that simple. The ultrasound technician is fully booked today, and you might have to come back in a few days with an appointment," he said. Like hell I was. There was no way I was going to let this man send me home without confirming the status of my child. Dead or alive, I deserved to know. He conceded and said we might have to wait a while. We waited.

Carla, the ultrasound technician, called us back into the ultrasound room. I was visibly upset, but she was so kind. She told me I needed to lay still, but I couldn't because I was so anxious that I was physically shaking. She turned the volume up and there it was again, that beautiful sound: PA-POW, PA-POW, PA-POW. At 162 bpm, the heart was strong. Our baby was just fine. Nuwan was so relieved that he was laughing from sheer joy. I started crying—again—but this time from unimaginable relief.

I wiped my tears and waited for the doctor to see us again. He said everything looked great, and then proceeded to lecture me for being upset.

"Do you know how many babies I've delivered? Over 10,000! Sometimes the device can't pick up the heartbeat at ten to twelve weeks."

I stopped him right there. "Doctor, do you know how many babies I've delivered? ZERO. This is my first child, and you declared that I had suffered a miscarriage without evidence and then commented on 'women *my* age'."

I stood my ground, and he stormed out of the room. It takes a special breed of despicable to be this insensitive towards a pregnant woman. I told Nuwan that I never wanted to see this doctor again.

• • •

The third obstetrician we saw was Dr. Haile, an unassuming physician with a warm smile. He shook hands with me as he introduced himself. My firm handshake impressed him, and he complimented me on it. He then saw a piece a paper sitting on the examination room table and asked if I had written questions on it. I said yes, front and back. "You must be an engineer," he correctly deduced.

Dr. Haile took a personal interest in answering all the questions thoroughly before starting the physical exam. When we finished, as I was about to get up, he extended his arm to me to help me. He was the first obstetrician to do that. And right there, I knew this was the man to deliver my child. I was acutely aware of the fact that we wouldn't actually get to choose our obstetrician, but that did not stop me from hoping. Maybe Dr. Haile would be on call the day I went into labor.

The following weekend Nuwan was mowing our lawn when he spotted a familiar face across the white picket fence, someone out mowing his own lawn. It was Dr. Haile! Nuwan was so excited by the coincidence that he came running into the house and woke me up. "Wake up, honey, our neighbor is Dr. Haile, and he's wearing an Ohio State sweatshirt!" I jumped out of bed along with my petite, melon-sized belly. I swiftly changed out of my pajamas, put on my red Ohio State hoodie, and ran out to say hello to Dr. Haile—also known as Ghalila's husband. Hallelujah, baby. Destiny at play again. We were neighbors with the most genuine, caring, and skilled obstetrician in town and his lovely wife. Little did I know that this relationship with our neighbor would play a pivotal role in bolstering us during the battle against cancer. But then again, my life is a culmination of brilliant coincidences and extraordinary twists of fate.

• • •

A few weeks later I noticed a pregnant woman across the street from us with her toddler daughter. She had always smiled at me, and that day I walked across to introduce myself. Her name was Emily, and she introduced me to her husband, Firas. They were a picture-perfect family. It was comforting to get to know more neighbors, and I started to feel more confident that we had made the right decision to move back.

My pregnancy progressed well, but I had some cardiac concerns, and the OB's office sent me to see a cardiologist. I was waiting nervously in a cold, dimly-lit room when a familiar face walked in. "Hi, I'm Dr. Ghanem...," he started. To which I reacted, "Firas, this is Niyati, your neighbor!" The rest of the appointment went swimmingly well. My cardiac issues were addressed, and it was determined that there was nothing wrong with me or the baby.

I knew I was in good hands: Firas across the street had my heart, and Dr. Haile next door had my pregnancy, delivery, and baby. I was set for life.

Dr. Haile insisted that we address him by his first name: Degaulle. This was such a humbling experience. I come from a land where doctors walk on water. This culture of humility is also a stark contrast from England. In the UK most people include all their credentials in work email signatures—their degrees and honors are spelled out. It seems too self-absorbed, if you ask me. To think we were with an obstetrician and cardiologist who insisted that we address each other by our first names felt like such a reprieve. Humanizing the physicians went a long way in helping me during my cancer treatment. I felt like I could relate to my doctors.

• • •

I loved being pregnant. I had a sign up in my cube, albeit a small one, that said, "I'm growing a human, what have you done today?" I was jokingly smug, and most of my work colleagues chuckled when they read the sign. I had a hard-to-miss, gargantuan belly that surpassed watermelons in size. Towards the end of my pregnancy, my bump was so high and enormous I could balance a plate on it. My two favorite activities were going for a swim and getting groceries. When I'd swim, the lifeguard on duty kept a close watch on me. He wanted to make sure I was safe as I waddled to the pool, swam a few laps, and floated around like a whale. Groceries were another highlight, because more often than not, when the store workers saw me, they would open a new checkout line, unload my groceries, and offer to load my car. I unabashedly enjoyed the preferential treatment. Women deserve accolades for the work we put in during gestation: taking care of our health, staying safe, and giving up some of our favorite foods and activities for the sake of the unborn child. While it's true that human beings have been doing this for time immemorial, and that producing offspring is intrinsic in nature, it doesn't make childbearing any less impressive. The act of growing a human, sustaining life inside of me, converting two cells into an entire being, seemed like a miracle.

• • •

At 4:30 a.m., thirty-six weeks and two days into my pregnancy, I had my first indisputable contraction. Want to know what it felt like? Like someone was stabbing me in the spine from the inside. Nuwan wondered if it was a Braxton Hicks contraction (aka a "fake" contraction). I gritted my teeth and said, "This is no false labor." I had been told contractions start off as cramps. CRAMPS? YOU CALL THIS CRAMPS? Well, let me tell you, this was all in the back, with excruciating pain, like nothing I've felt before and nothing any man will ever experience. (Don't even *think* of comparing it to being kicked in the balls.)

We raced to the hospital. Eight minutes of hell later we were there. We abandoned our car at the main entrance of the hospital in a complete state of panic, and Nuwan rushed inside to find a wheelchair. Do other expecting parents do this: drive to the hospital, ditch the car, and sprint to delivery? My water broke. Nuwan was gleaming with joy. "Honey, we are going to have the baby!" I was petrified. Degaulle came in, all calm and collected, like it was nothing he hadn't seen before. And it wasn't.

The anesthesiologist gave me an epidural. Given the rapid progression of my labor, I was minutes away from it being too late for one, but I lucked out. The epidural is a godsend. The man who invented it must have been a woman. After this the labor nurses did an amazing job of coaching me how to push. Degaulle kept encouraging me. Nuwan was so proud of me already, but I knew we were both a little scared. Degaulle made some joke about the Ohio State-Michigan rivalry to lighten the mood; I wanted to smack him but was too exhausted. Nuwan made small talk, and I wanted to smack him too. Three hours and forty minutes later I delivered a healthy baby boy weighing six pounds and two ounces, with a full head of hair and strong lungs. (Lungs are the last organ to develop and the biggest concern when it comes to premature babies, so this was a huge relief.) Nuwan was over the moon. He was a proud father. Degaulle handed the surgical scissors to Nuwan, and he cut the umbilical cord. Degaulle said he wasn't surprised that I had delivered this quickly. "Like everything else about you, you have an overachieving uterus," he said, finally getting me to laugh. You see, with contractions done and a baby in my arms, jokes were funny again. I thanked Degaulle for delivering my son. I'll never forget his response: "It is my honor."

• • •

The moment I saw my baby boy, there was such a flood of overwhelming joy and love that I felt my heart would explode. I did not know that I was capable of loving someone so much and so instantaneously. To promote breastfeeding they put the baby on my chest minutes after he was born, and while he was there, I studied his anatomy. It was the miracle of life: a real human child, with ten fingers and ten toes, two eyes and a nose, and beautiful rosy lips. We named him Vihaan Rajendra Gallege. *Vihaan* means "the first light of dawn", which is exactly when he was born. Rajendra is my father's first name, and Gallege is my husband's last name.

Childbirth gave me a whole new appreciation for my body. Before it, I didn't know how strong I was and what my body was capable of. This memory of my son's birth was a source of strength during the cancer treatment.

I quickly found out that breastfeeding is hard work. It didn't feel innate but rather like a learned skill for Vihaan and me. Vihaan went through bouts of cluster feeding, which is when the baby continues to feed for hours, from one side to the other. One evening, two-month-old Vihaan cluster fed from 9:30 p.m. to 1:30 a.m.! The mantra I kept hearing was, "You're not producing enough milk." The more I was doubted, though, the more resolute I was to make breastfeeding work. I had never been so determined before. I took an oath: "No matter how exhausted, sleep-deprived, or unwell I am, I will breastfeed my child." I did not supplement with formula. I was a full-time working mother, who made breastfeeding work, and no, it wasn't easy. But this is what I'm made of.

• • •

Nuwan was nervous about having a second child, and rightfully so. He remembered how hard it was the first time around with Vihaan, the sleepless nights and incessant breastfeeding. Our life had just started to settle into a new routine, and Vihaan was somewhat manageable by now. We each had our own set of pros and cons when it came to the decision; maybe we should wait longer, maybe we should stop at one. Nuwan eventually conceded, as all good sperm donors do. Like magic, I was pregnant again. This time around I took the pregnancy test on Father's Day. It was my Father's Day present to Nuwan. He was overjoyed! The same evening I knocked on Ghalila and Degaulle's door. Degaulle opened and asked me to come in.

"Would you like a beer?"

"Degaulle, we are pregnant! I'm having another baby," I said.

"Water for you, beer for me!" he replied with a gleam in his eye.

Every day I prayed, "Please let it be a girl. Healthy baby, but baby girl." The week-twenty anatomy scan revealed that I was, in fact, having a GIRL! *Thank you, Krishna, Hare Krishna!* Degaulle delivered her, too, and the delivery was even faster this time. From start of contractions to a baby in my arms, the delivery took a staggering two hours and twenty minutes. My overachieving uterus did it again! We named her Aarini Niyati Gallege, *Aarini* meaning "adventurous" in Sanskrit. Aarini was placed on my bare chest almost as soon as she was born, and Nuwan cut the umbilical cord. I couldn't take my eyes off her. At thirty-seven weeks she was a full-term baby and weighed nearly seven pounds. Aarini was perfect, and my heart exploded with joy all over again.

When Degaulle was leaving the hospital room, I said to him—and I distinctly remember this— "Degaulle, the world is an infinitely better place with you in it."

• • •

The miracle of life, they call it, and it truly is a miracle. The birth of my two children is the closest I have felt to God. I cannot explain it, but there is something about that moment when the baby comes out that is spellbinding and so pure; this was the most honest, incorruptible moment of my life. And to think I had the opportunity to do it twice. As with Vihaan, breastfeeding empowered me. I was using my breasts for the one and only purpose God intended: to provide food for my babies.

I am grateful that I was in the right frame of mind to cherish childbirth. I cherish that Nuwan and I had five glorious years of marriage under our belt before having children. I am thankful that we were financially stable. I am filled with gratitude that we didn't have trouble conceiving, and that we had healthy children.

Throughout my cancer treatment, no matter how tired or sick I was, the sound of their giggles filled my heart. I wanted to protect their innocence, to give them an opportunity to explore and grow into good human beings. I feel no greater joy than that given by my children, and no greater pride than seeing them prosper and thrive. They are the greatest gift God has given us and my biggest source of strength, no questions asked.

5. TREATMENT PLAN

"She has the gift of accepting her life."
— Jhumpa Lahiri, *The Namesake*

The day I was diagnosed I called, texted, and messaged most of my family and friends. Even though I was in shock, my mind started to focus on two things: 1) what came next, and 2) what was important to me. In terms of my medical treatment, I had to be patient. Tumor pathology can take weeks. I figured that if I focused on achievable short-term and long-term goals, it would create a sense of control in a world where I felt completely overwhelmed. It was how I coped.

I knew the first and most important thing was for my children to remember me as I was, right at the time of the diagnosis, with my whole body intact and my beautiful long hair. I emailed Amanda, a professional photographer friend who had recently done maternity and baby pictures for us. My message was succinct: "I've been diagnosed with breast cancer. I need family pictures, and I need them soon, before they decide on chemotherapy and mastectomy plans." I called in a favor. Amanda wrote back within minutes of reading the email. We talked over the phone and set up a time to do a photoshoot at home.

Amanda did this pro bono. *Short-term achievable goal, check.* If I could just smile through my worries and fight those tears, I thought, my children would have something to remember me by. I wanted them to remember me with my luscious long hair, slender body, and bright smile. And that's just what Nuwan and I did: we smiled and laughed as we did a lifestyle photoshoot at home with both the kids. Amanda captured a poignant moment of me breastfeeding my daughter. She asked me to look up and smile, but I had tears in my eyes. I look gutted in those. I was not able to hide my fears. Amanda gave us close to one hundred pictures. Nuwan and I chose our favorite and framed a massive picture for our living room.

Another short-term achievable goal quickly presented itself. I was diagnosed on a Friday, and the following Monday I was scheduled to attend a three-day Women in Technology conference organized by my company. Only the top tier of women engineers get invited to this conference, and I was one of them. It was an elite group of 110 women from all different parts of the company. There was an impressive lineup of speakers, panel discussions, workshops, and face-to-face time with executive leadership. I had two options: sit at home and contemplate mortality, or put on a brave face and attend the conference. I attended the conference. This is how hardcore I am. I took time out of the conference to go for an MRI and a physician's consult. But I was not MIA and did not skip the conference. Nor did I attend in disguise. I told my colleagues that I had been diagnosed with breast cancer. When they asked what stage, what the treatment plan was, etc., I told them I didn't have answers yet. I was a breastfeeding mother with a thirteen-month-old baby and a four-year-old son and a dedicated husband gearing up for the toughest fight of my life. Cancer wasn't going to take this conference away from me.

My mind wandered during the event. I went through the list of possibilities: chemotherapy, hair loss, the potential loss of one breast—but if I'm lucky, a lumpectomy, or a bit of radiation. All this and I should be back on my feet. Figuring out the treatment was the critical next step. While Nuwan and I hoped for the least severe treatment, I prepared for the worst. I had a feeling that we were in for a rough ride. Even with all these thoughts racing through my mind, I wanted to be present and participating at the conference. So, I raised my hand, asked questions, and mingled with my peers. Several of the role models and leaders I look up to saw me break down. But this news was so hard on us, and such a shock, how could I not?

Nuwan was proud of me for attending and participating in the conference. He said it was a great show of strength. I didn't want the cancer diagnosis to terminate my career—I wanted to prove to myself that I could handle this, and I would do so by working. It was my way of saying, "Screw you!" to the cancer.

I was bitter about the hand we were dealt, and it translated into unkind comments on my part. After the diagnosis I started cursing—at work, at home, during my doctor's appointments. If there is one time you're permitted to curse, this has to be it. When a colleague told me her father-in-law had cancer, I snapped back and asked, "Is your father-in-law a breastfeeding mother of two?" Another friend said to me, "I know how hard this is; my mother and aunt had it." How could she have known how hard this was? That conversation just made me mad. All these people trying to empathize boiled my blood. because in my mind, they were doing a rubbish job of it. I wanted to say out loud, "You don't understand how hard this is." Like I said, I was bitter about the hand fate had dealt us. And that translated into my mean-spirited responses. I realize now that they were trying to be supportive. I should have just graciously listened or nodded. But I wasn't in the right frame of mind.

I fought back tears as I told my senior managers Joan and Cathy about my diagnosis. During a conversation with Joan, I said, "Joan, I'm devastated about losing my breasts. My children still jump into the shower with me. No breasts will be traumatic for them."

"Children are resilient, Niyati; all they want is you."

That hit home. Kids are incredibly resilient. I had that going for me, because Vihaan and Aarini were young.

Gary, the executive director of the business unit I work for, was devastated when he found out about my diagnosis. He asked me if we could talk in private for a few minutes. We found an open conference room. I told Gary about the hellish week Nuwan and I had had, and how this nightmare had turned into our reality. I cried as I said, "Gary, I have two children. I have to be around for them." He had tears in his eyes. He shared his story about loved ones getting diagnosed with breast cancer, and said it was hard on the family, but they got through it. Maybe that's what I wanted to hear, to have someone to validate my fears. I didn't want to hear, "Stay positive, be strong." To heck with positive. I had breast cancer.

Nuwan was worried senseless about me during the conference, which was a closed-door event. He found a desk outside the main meeting room and worked from there during the entire conference, just so he wouldn't be too far away from me. It melts my heart just thinking about it. Love like this is immeasurable.

With two short-term goals tackled, I wanted to keep my mind occupied with a longer-term goal that would serve as a distraction. The goal came easily to me: at the end of treatment, I wanted to go with Nuwan and the kids on a holiday, to go somewhere unique. The location had to be the Galapagos Islands, no questions asked! It was somewhere I wanted to spend our honeymoon, and it had been on my list of places to visit for a while. This vacation would require a lot of planning, a tight budget, lots of child-friendly options, and the courage to take two little ones to such remote islands. I was about to go through chemotherapy and surgery; courage I had, and money would cover the rest.

• • •

Things started to unravel quickly, however, as my pathology reports came back. My tumor type was aggressive. Given my young age, the oncologist, breast surgeon, and radiation oncologist all wanted to treat me with a plan that would give me the best shot at survival. I was overwhelmed, and desperately needed someone to help us navigate the convoluted healthcare system.

In the United States, no one is in charge of your cancer treatment. During my pregnancies, the obstetrician was in charge of my care and delivering the baby. When I go to work, the chief engineer is in charge of developing an engine into production. If you're the boss, there's a team you can delegate to; or, if you're the minion, there's a boss who will guide you. But the cancer journey is complicated. There's no "chief physician"—each expert attends to his or her responsibility, does due diligence, and then hands the patient over to the next savant.

It took less than forty-eight hours after the diagnosis for me and Nuwan to realize that we were in over our heads. I called Degaulle in yet another moment of desperation and asked, "Who's in charge?" He told me I was. How was that possible? How was I supposed to navigate the complex world of oncology and make life-and-death decisions for myself? Nuwan and I knew nothing about cancer, and yet we were supposed to pick out doctors from a pile of experts around us. Each physician inundated us with information, pamphlets, and a flurry of options. My brain went into software programming mode, if-then-else statements, and flowcharts. *If the tumor is small and within one quadrant of the breast, then I'll get a lumpectomy, or else, mastectomy. If it is a single mastectomy, then we'll consider a prophylactic double mastectomy.*

Degaulle understood how overwhelming this experience was. He said, "Niyati, I will take care of everything. I will help you get appointments and your physicians aligned." And he did just that. He recommended Dr. Zusan for my breast surgery, Dr. Wagner for oncology, and Dr. McMullen for radiation.

Our first meeting with Dr. Zusan was nerve-racking. I was sick to my stomach. No, really—I was nauseous, and my legs went numb in the waiting room. Nuwan and I waited for what seemed like an eternity. Nuwan helped me take my boots off and started to massage my legs and feet. I felt like I was going to throw up. The waiting—a mix of anticipation and that sick-to-the-stomach feeling—is the most excruciating part of having cancer. They can medicate for pain and nausea, but for this level of anxiety—anxiety that turns your stomach into knots—there is no antidote. As we sat there, I prayed that Dr. Zusan would tell us she could do a lumpectomy, and that I would get to keep my breasts. I did not want to lose them. Nuwan was hopeful, but a cloud of dread hung over us.

Dr. Zusan was a tenderhearted young woman who saw herself in me. She had two young children of her own. She had the impossible job of describing my treatment plan and the long road ahead for us. When we met her, Nuwan and I did not know the extent of the cancer. In my mind I was still bargaining: *maybe I can keep the breast, maybe I will only need radiation therapy*. Then Dr. Zusan broke the news to us: there was no saving the breast. And chemotherapy would be needed, along with radiation. I was in for the deluxe treatment for cancer, the whole package.

My mind wandered in and out of shock as she described the treatment plan. I told Nuwan that I couldn't put the children through this, that I needed to move out of the house for a year to get treatment. "Absolutely not, darling. We are in this together," he said. I shuddered at the thought of losing my hair, my eyebrows, and eyelashes. Cancer patients look like cancer patients because of the unmistakable baldness.

My body went numb when Dr. Zusan said it would have to be a

mastectomy. I was going to lose my left breast. I was in tears; Nuwan was too. I said to her, "Dr. Zusan, please can you just help me die? I don't want to go through this. I want to die." Her eyes welled up, and her cheeks flushed. She held my hand and said, "I cannot let you do that. We will get through this. This time next year, all this will be behind us. You have a loving husband and two children. We cannot let you do that." Dr. Zusan is an angel. Or what we say in Hindi, a *farishta*, which originates from a Persian word for "angel". It's no surprise Dr. Zusan is a breast surgeon. Even in this dark moment, I was so thankful to Degaulle for recommending that I see her.

The plan was to get neoadjuvant chemotherapy. That's a fancy way of saying, "Chemo before surgery." I didn't know much about cancer, but I had always thought the tumor should be removed first. Get the tumor out before it spreads even more, and then treat the remnants with chemotherapy. When I spoke to family and friends in India, they, too, were surprised by this plan. Dr. Zusan explained the science behind it: "We need to know how the tumor reacts to chemotherapy. We expect the tumors to shrink. This not only gives us better margins while performing surgery, but also proves to us if the cocktail of chemotherapy worked. If you take the tumor out first, then you don't know how effective chemotherapy has been."

Nuwan asked why I needed radiation at the end of all of this. Dr. Zusan explained that even after surgery, there can be microscopic cells that get left behind, cells that might be resistant to the chemotherapy. Radiation targets the suspect cancer regions of the body to ensure that rogue cancer cells are destroyed. "It's like an insurance policy," she said.

Dr. Zusan spent three hours with us. She listed potential cancer types and how treatment is chosen based on tumor pathology. She was thorough and wrote everything down for us, and even drew diagrams. The patience and empathy she showed us were extraordinary. We were overwhelmed, but tried hard to get our heads around the treatment. Towards the end of the appointment, Nuwan again teared up as Dr. Zusan was examining me. Seeing him distraught brought tears to her eyes, and she hugged him. She had so much compassion for us. Where else in the world would you find a physician, who doesn't know you from Adam, showing this much compassion? I'm not sure, to be honest. I had always thought that doctors don't have time to hug and cry with patients. They are untouchable and walk on water. But Dr. Zusan had just shattered this notion. Without a shadow of a doubt, I knew in that moment that this was the best possible place to get the worst possible news of our life.

Nuwan and I were drained of all energy after the appointment, but at the same time a cloud had lifted. We knew the path ahead. The journey ahead felt insurmountable, but it was the journey that life had dealt us. I called my sister in India after the appointment, from the hospital waiting room. With the time difference I reached Priya in the wee hours of the morning. But at this point she had stopped sleeping; none of us slept anymore. She was waiting on edge by the phone. I told her it was going to be chemotherapy, mastectomy, then radiation. She was devastated. She was praying hard for me, praying it would not be chemotherapy. She had recently watched a loved one go through it, and it had been dreadful. But this was our reality. Without a doubt in her mind, Priya said, "I'm coming to the US. I will be there to help you, Nuwan, and the kids. No matter what it takes." I love my sister so much. Her heart was bleeding for me. I don't deserve her.

Nuwan and I talked about the cancer treatment on the drive back from Dr. Zusan's office. With my left breast ravaged by this disease, I asked Nuwan, what was the point of keeping the right one? It's a ticking time bomb. My cancer was aggressive, and we were lucky that breastfeeding helped me detect the tumor as early as I had. What were the odds that the disease would rear its ugly head on the right side? What were the chances I would get lucky and detect it in time on the right side, and that it wouldn't kill me? The answer was clear and irrefutable to me: I was going to opt for a bilateral mastectomy. Get rid of both sides and give myself the best chance of survival. I had to live to see my children grow up. The decision was made—a double mastectomy it would be.

6. THE DECIMATOR

**"You think you are the greatest sufferer
in the world?"**
— Chinua Achebe, *Things Fall Apart*

The next piece of the puzzle was determining the type of chemotherapy and how many cycles I would need. Degaulle scheduled us to meet with an oncologist named Dr. Wagner, who would help us do just that. As we waited nervously in the oncology examination room, I felt a familiar pit in my stomach. I was nauseous again. Nuwan tried to help the circulation around my legs and got down on the floor to massage me and help ease my anxiety. Dr. Wagner walked in the room with her sidekick, a nurse navigator named Kim.

Dr. Wagner did not believe in sugarcoating things or fudging the facts. Unpleasantness was her reality, day in and day out, as she took care of cancer patients. She told us statistics, the prognosis, and the horrendous side effects of chemotherapy. She told me that managing side effects was important to her, and that she would help preempt them. She told me that I would lose my hair, all of it. I was crushed.

Dr. Wagner explained that cancer cells, unlike normal cells, grow uncontrollably. Chemotherapy drugs work by attacking whatever fast-dividing cells it finds in the body, with the aim of destroying all the cancer cells. But there's collateral damage. Rapidly dividing healthy cells such as hair follicles, nails, the gastrointestinal tract, the mouth and throat, and—most crucially—the bone marrow get affected too. The reason why cancer patients are immunocompromised is partly because chemotherapy causes a drop in white blood cells, making them prone to infections. Chemotherapy decimates everything in its wake. It's essentially the art of administering just enough poison not to kill the patient.

Upon hearing this, I was immediately concerned about my biggest asset. Did you just think I meant my hair? Lord, no—my BRAIN. If chemotherapy attacks organs, cells, and everything else, what happens to the brain? Dr. Wagner told me there's a phenomenon known as "chemo brain." She described it as feeling foggy, not being as sharp or alert. To which I said, "So, I'll finally know what it's like to be above average?" Dr. Wagner and Kim laughed so hard that I'm sure the rest of the cancer center heard the cackle. "She's my kind of people," said Dr. Wagner, looking at Kim. "You can call me Stephanie." We were now on a first-name basis.

"That's my wife," said Nuwan. He was so proud of me for finding humor in this darkest of moments.

I told all three of them, "Look, if during chemotherapy I lose my wicked sense of humor, then you will know something is really wrong. Let this be the gold standard of normalcy when you gauge how I'm doing with the treatment." More laughter. Sometimes I think I should seriously consider stand-up comedy as a side gig. Humor is my coping mechanism. The day I lose the ability to laugh is the day I have lost the essence of life.

Towards the end of our otherwise serious conversation I commented to Stephanie, admittedly naïvely, "You know I'm going to beat this, right?"

She got serious again, and said this was not something she says to any of her patients, adding that there's still much about cancer we don't know. She also said she wouldn't be surprised if, at this point, I was in Stage 4 of the disease, because of the aggressive nature of my tumor.

It was sobering to hear that. I was disheartened, but I knew she didn't believe in giving false hope and was a woman of principle. Whatever happened that day at the appointment, whether it was my wit or her candor, my optimism in the face of adversity, or her brutal honesty, something clicked between us. Stephanie wrote down her cellphone number and had Kim give it to us. I was surprised by the gesture. It took me just one meeting with my oncologist to score her personal cellphone number. I've got mad skills, people! Sarcasm is my second language, and I think Stephanie could relate to that. We got on like a house on fire (that's some British slang for you). I am so grateful Degaulle recommended that I see Stephanie. I was two-for-two. With Dr. Zusan and Stephanie on my side, I was in good hands.

• • •

I needed minor surgery before we could start chemotherapy. I'll explain. Chemotherapy is administered intravenously, and the process can take a few hours depending on the dosage. Back in the day, patients were poked in the arm with a needle for each session. This caused all kinds of problems: collapsed veins, bruised veins, or the drug itself spilling out. Chemotherapy drugs are so toxic, though, that if they come in contact with tissue, they will destroy it irreparably. Eventually a genius came up with a new method of administering the drugs that involves connecting a portable catheter to the body's largest vein, which goes directly to the right atrium of the heart (the upper-right chamber). This helps ensure that the drugs are dispensed repeatedly and safely. Dr. Zusan explained that veins coming from the heart are like the roots of a tree, thick and large. As you go towards the extremities the veins get smaller. Thus targeting the largest vein directly ensures a clear route for the drugs. (Isn't it great when a physician can explain things in layman's terms?) To secure the connection, a device known as a "port-a-cath" is implanted under the skin of the chest. While all this sounds sophisticated, I told Nuwan, "Great, they will just inject poison directly into my heart. Nothing could possibly go wrong there."

Despite my morbid jokes, this little device was a lifesaver. The port-a-cath gave the cancer center staff easy access to draw blood and to administer chemotherapy drugs. They also gave me a topical numbing cream, so that when it came time to get poked and prodded, I would feel no pain. I appreciated that they didn't want me to feel the poke of a needle.

I am so grateful that cancer care in this country takes a patient's pain and suffering into account. I know from loved ones who have gone through cancer treatment in India that symptom management isn't given as much importance. The US healthcare system, as far as cancer treatment is concerned, gives paramount importance to patient comfort. It's a testament to the empathy of cancer care providers. More importantly, a huge value is put on catching things before the patient's condition worsens. For example, I was given a shot twenty-four hours after each individual chemotherapy treatment, to help stimulate my bone marrow to produce white blood cells (WBCs). This shot was a preemptive measure to make sure my WBCs didn't get too low. In India, cancer patients are monitored, but only when their white blood count dips to dangerously low levels are they given the shot. It's not as though medical knowledge and specialized drugs don't exist in India. Regardless, I feel this approach provides a disservice to the patients, because by the time the WBCs plummet, they will be vulnerable to infections and have weakened immune systems, which could cause other complications. Why wait? Preempt it.

Nuwan argued that things are practiced differently in India because the array of drugs I was on are cost-prohibitive. There's some truth to it. The

Neulasta shot to stimulate my bone marrow cost $11,000—per shot! But I think there's more to it than the money aspect. I'll give you an example. Most, if not all, chemotherapy patients suffer from painful mouth sores. To help with this, oncologists in the US prescribe this incredible mouthwash called magic mouthwash. And, boy, let me tell you, it is magic. This mouthwash is made up of a combination of antibacterial, antifungal, anesthetic, and anti-inflammatory ingredients. Swish it around a couple times a day and the mouth sores are manageable. With Stephanie's magic mouthwash, I was even able to eat spicy curries. And this is not an expensive compound. On the other hand, an aunt in India who was undergoing chemotherapy suffered from agonizing mouth sores, and she was treated at the top cancer hospital in the country, Tata Memorial Hospital in Mumbai. Yet there was no magic mouthwash.

• • •

I was scheduled for my port-a-cath surgery on March 13, eleven days after my initial diagnosis. More important than the surgery, though, was what we had scheduled beforehand. I was due to get a PET scan to determine if the cancer had spread through my body. The night before I couldn't sleep. I texted my sister, telling her I felt like I was drowning. Maybe it was a panic attack; I'm not sure. But I *did* feel like I was drowning, and I was physically gasping for air. I was sick to my stomach. The PET scan would be crucial for determining my future.

My tumor was aggressive. Every tumor has a measurable protein called Ki67. It's measured as a percentage: the higher the Ki67 percentage, the more aggressive the tumor. It's hoped that a Ki67 number is lower than 10 percent, as anything above that threshold is considered high. But you know me by now: I like to outperform. I am an overachiever. Indeed, my Ki67 number was 96 percent. Hence the concern, "Has the cancer spread?"

At this point I had been designated Stage 3C. The worrying thing was that the more tests we did, the worse my staging got. There was no improvement in the clinical staging. There was a possibility that I had been at Stage 2 when the biopsy results were received, but that went out the window with the MRI results. The MRI found a third tumor in my breast, and this, combined with the cancer in my lymph nodes, gave me a Stage 3 status. This is what was on my mind before the PET scan. Yet again, I was sick to my stomach. The PET scan needed to show no spread of the disease. *Needed to.* I told Nuwan, "I am willing to fight this disease. I'll take the chemotherapy, they can have my breasts, I'll do whatever radiation is needed. But only if I know there's a chance at survival. Stage 4 is bleak, and I am not ready for that."

We prayed for the bad news to stop here. Nuwan was confident that it would. Priya prayed profusely and told me, "God is not that unkind. We have been through more than our share of hardship. This will not be our reality. The PET scan will come out clean."

My sister has unwavering faith in God. I prayed too, but I have this irrational belief that Priya's prayers are purer and more likely to be heard.

The hospital told me that the PET scan can take a couple days to be read, which I was dismayed to hear. I called the nurse navigator and said, "I'm a thirty-four-year-old woman with two small children at home. I deserve to know the results sooner. Please see if you can get the radiologist to read my scans on the same day. Please." She said she would pass on the message. I guess my pleading worked, because the radiologist read my scans the same day. After the PET scan I was taken to the surgery preparation room. Nuwan and I waited there nervously. Before they took me in, the nurse navigator came in with a sealed envelope with my results. She had a guarded smile on her face as she said, "Your results are clear." What a profound relief! This was the best news to get before going in for a surgery. Nuwan and I kissed each other. I called Priya and Vikram *dada*.

Other than the cancer sites that we were already aware of, the PET scan was clear. Thank you, God.

While Nuwan and I were waiting for the surgery to start, in came a young-looking fella. "Hi, I'm Dr. Payne, I'll be your anesth . . ." wait, *what*? The man in charge of ensuring I felt no pain was named Dr. PAYNE. This poor kid was probably mocked his entire residency. But this was not the time for kindness. I seized the opportunity, teasing him about his name and his youth. What can I say? I like to go out with a bang.

In all fairness, I have to tell you how sweet Dr. Payne was. I told him I'm blind as a bat, and I know I need to remove my glasses before surgery, but not being able to see my surgeon and the room clearly would really make me nervous. I asked him if he could leave my glasses on till I was out, and then make sure they were back on before I woke up. He said that he would be happy to make my experience as comfortable as possible. I then told him that I have a terrible gag reflex, and since they were going to intubate me, I asked him if he could make sure to pull the device out of my mouth before I come out of anesthesia completely; he said that he would.

When we went into the operating room, he asked me what I worked on. I started to explain, "91-liter natural gas engines, these engines are used . . .", and just like that, I was out. I remember waking up as they got me prepped for a chest x-ray, to ensure the catheter was placed correctly. I had my glasses on, and I saw Nuwan. *Thank you, Dr. Payne*. It's the little things that go a long way. Sometimes people lose sight of this. You don't need to organize a massive fundraiser or twenty hours of community service to be appreciated. Even the smallest acts of kindness can have a profound impact.

• • •

I asked a few close cousins if they could come over to help during chemotherapy. I worried about how I would look to them, bald and fatigued. I cringed at the thought of my relatives seeing me ill. But I needed help, and this was the price I would have to pay. I was told that I was brave for enduring it all. But I didn't feel brave; I felt like the treatments stripped me of my dignity. I wished I could have avoided asking for help altogether, but I needed it. I made one rule, though: other than my cousin Vikram, there would be no men in the house. Vikram holds a special place in my life and is very dear to me. He is also a doctor for whom I have immense respect.

I handed over the responsibility of coordinating help from the family to my first cousin Apurva. She is a master planner and one of the most compassionate people I know. Between Apurva and Catharine, my cousin Prashant's wife, they were able move heaven and earth to make sure we had help. I reached out to both of them in moments of desperation, expressing how overwhelmed I felt. The entire experience of being sick was exhausting, never mind the sickness itself. I had made a calendar of events and appointments, some of which were officially scheduled, like chemotherapy sessions, and some of which were estimated dates and guesses. Apurva and Catharine took charge, based only on this preliminary calendar. They had us covered every other week. Thanks to my cousins and aunts, I had help with childcare, errands, and the important task of being there for me during a chemotherapy cycle. They also lined up backups for unforeseen circumstances such as illness and flight cancellations.

Apurva lives in Connecticut and Catharine in Manhattan. They both have toddler sons, whom they left behind with their husbands, so that they could come to Columbus and help me and Nuwan with the children and my chemotherapy.

I didn't have to call a single aunt or cousin to coordinate calendars and schedules. I had not one, but two Super Women on my team. All the husbands also stepped up, feeding and watering the kids and keeping their homes running. This is MY family. The Koli-Tamaskar clan sticks together. And for that I am so proud to be a Tamaskar.

• • •

In preparation for the first round of chemotherapy, my friend Katie took me to a salon for a haircut. This was a nice gesture, but the end was near; I knew I would soon lose it all. In anticipation I cut my waist-long hair down to a shorter, shoulder-length cut.

The evening before my first chemotherapy session, my son was sent home from daycare because of a fever. Nuwan took him to the pediatrician's office, and Vihaan tested positive for the flu! In a moment of panic, I got in the car and started heading to the local urgent care to get tested myself. I was afraid that if I had the flu, Stephanie would not be able to start my chemo. I cautiously texted Stephanie, not wanting to take advantage of her kindness. I feared she would regret sharing her number with us, given that I had texted her *before* chemotherapy even started. She called me back and told me not to even bother going to urgent care. She prescribed Tamiflu, an antiviral medicine that helps alleviate symptoms of the flu, for both Nuwan and me. Our pediatrician, Dr. Harris, prescribed Tamiflu for Vihaan and Aarini. The whole house was taking Tamiflu a day before chemo started.

The first day of chemotherapy was a good one. Nuwan and I were happy to get started. Yes, you heard me: happy. Not because we thought the session was going to be fun, but because this was our first step towards attacking the cancer that had invaded my body. I told Stephanie that, if I had had an option, I would've started chemo yesterday. Each day I waited for results or to figure out a game plan was a day that cancer was winning. So yes, the first chemotherapy session was a happy occasion for us. I remember the date: March 14, less than twenty-four hours after my port-a-cath surgery. I hope you have no doubt about how badass I am.

Stephanie prescribed a cocktail of three chemotherapy drugs for me: Adriamycin and Cytoxan, followed by Taxol. Each drug she prescribed attacks cancer cells differently. Adriamycin slows down the growth of cancer cells, and Cytoxan damages the genetic makeup of the cancer cells. Cytoxan given with Adriamycin is known as "dose-dense AC chemotherapy," a combination that's been found to increase the efficacy of both drugs. And finally, Taxol causes disruption in the cell division phase. These are nonmedical descriptions of the drugs, of course. We were curious as to why I needed three drugs and what each did, so we asked a lot of questions.

Adriamycin is infamously known as the "red devil." This drug had to be injected into my vein manually, not through an intravenous bag, which is how the other drugs were given. It was red in color, and the oncology nurse, wearing two sets of gloves, took more than ten minutes to push it one milliliter at a time. Each time the nurse pushed the drug in, she pulled blood out, to ensure that there was good blood flow, and that the vein wasn't compromised. Adriamycin is notorious for causing tissue damage if not administered properly, and is also known to cause long-term cardiac concerns. (They call it "cardiotoxicity".) Before the red devil, I was given a bag of steroids, anti-nausea medicine, and a combination of anti-inflammatory and pain medicine. The combination of all that intravenous fluid, coupled with me downing several bottles of water, meant I was ready to go to the bathroom as soon as they were done with the infusion. I was shocked that within minutes of getting this toxic drug my pee turned red, blood red. *That's not disconcerting at all.* I'm sure you didn't want to read this, but I want to drive home how potent the drugs are. It took more than twenty-four hours for me to pee normally again. All right, I'm done; no more talk of human effluent.

A strange thing happened during that first infusion of Adriamycin: I felt a tingling in my tumor. I kid you not. It wasn't a placebo; it wasn't just in my head—it was palpable. When I felt it, I immediately told Nuwan, "Honey, I feel tingling in the tumor. It is like the chemo is working!" It was such a strange feeling, because the tumor was otherwise felt dormant, insensitive to any sensation. And now I could feel its presence. Or should I say its destruction? I told Stephanie about this experience, too. That tingling around the tumor site didn't happen again during the rest of my treatment.

The first twenty-four hours after chemotherapy, I felt normal. It was the magic of steroids. I was mentally drained, but physically felt just fine. By day two, however, the symptoms hit me like a ton of bricks. I was nauseous and fatigued. That second day I was asked to return to the hospital to get my first shot of Neulasta. The shot itself isn't painful, but the suffering afterwards is agonizing. My shoulder blades and upper back started to hurt. It was a deep, agonizing bone pain. My femurs started to hurt the same way, from deep within. No amount of pain medicine or muscle relaxants could help with this ache. Fatigue, nausea, and bone pain combined to make me miserable. But I knew there was one thing that would help. Other than keeping on top of my anti-nausea drugs, steroid pills, and multivitamins (of course), I needed to keep my mind occupied. So I worked. That's how I chemo'ed: laptop open, calling in to meetings, working.

We had a lot of help during that first chemotherapy session. Aai, Apurva, Catharine, and Nuwan all worked around the clock to help with childcare, tasks around the house, cooking, and charting symptoms. Stephanie had told us that, for the most part, the side effects repeat themselves in a cyclical manner. Thus what I experienced during the first session would be a good predictor for the following ones. Apurva made a spreadsheet plotting the nausea, fatigue, and body aches and pains against the drugs I was taking. This gave us a good idea of what was working and what wasn't, and helped us keep on top of the nausea.

We had a full house of help again for my second round of chemotherapy. I had my mother, Vikram, Beena, their daughter Arya, and Catharine over. After that second session, I noticed that each time I ran my hand through my hair, chunks came out. I was losing my hair, and it was soul-crushing. I booked an appointment for another haircut. This time Catharine and Arya came with me to the salon. The stylist, Ashley, asked, "What are you thinking about doing today?" as she ran her hands through my hair, and everything became obvious to her.

"I'm going through chemotherapy at the moment, and I'm losing my hair. I need you to cut it really short."

She choked up, and said, "Let's get you a nice scalp massage and shampoo first."

It was the quietest salon appointment I've ever had. Neither of us spoke. Ashley then asked if I wanted my head shaved. I told her I just wanted it shorter, so that when the hair fell off, it wouldn't be as messy and dramatic. As she started to cut my hair short, I had tears in my eyes. It was devastating. Devastating to go from having hair down to my waist to a haircut that made me look like a boy. I had never sported short hair in my life; from the time I was a baby, once my hair grew out, I had always had long hair. By the time I was five I had hair down to my waist. I maintained different lengths, but had long hair all my life. Cutting and partly shaving my hair marked the end of all this.

When we got done I couldn't look at myself in the mirror. I had tears in my eyes. Arya, my sweet, darling niece, said, "Niyati *aatya*, you look beautiful." Catharine echoed that. I went to pay for my haircut, but at the checkout, the receptionist said, "Ashley doesn't want to charge you for this." I was in tears yet again. I grabbed a twenty from my wallet (all I had), gave it to Catharine, and told her to give Ashley a tip. Catharine went and spoke to Ashley. Through tears, she said she didn't want to accept the money. I insisted from across the room that she take it. Ashley reluctantly accepted the tip. I knew right then that my cancer had hit home for her. There must be a story behind her reaction, and her empathy left me humbled. There is so much kindness in this world. It is unfortunate that it took this cancer to help me see it. But I see it everywhere now—more kindness than hate, more empathy than indifference.

The days at the hospital were long. I went from bloodwork to a physician consult to chemotherapy. The better we got at preempting symptoms, though, the more manageable chemotherapy became. Stephanie is a brilliant oncologist, and she helped me to adapt after each new round of symptoms. When my nausea and fatigue got to a point that I just couldn't handle, she advised IV therapy. She told me to come into the hospital and get two liters of intravenous saline. In her experience, IV therapy doesn't just hydrate the patient, it helps with nausea, too. Well, it worked for me. I felt energized, and my nausea all but disappeared. We continued that regimen for the first four cycles, which were particularly rough on the body.

At one of my chemotherapy appointments, when Kim asked about my symptoms, I sheepishly said, "I have it logged here," and showed her the spreadsheet Apurva had made. It had eight days of symptoms and a list of what medicines helped me. This spreadsheet was so thorough that Kim wanted a copy of it. I removed my personal information and shared it with her. She wanted to use it with some of her older patients.

Before too long I lost all my hair. It just came right off. I retained my eyebrows and lashes, but the hair on my head was gone. By the time I lost it, I had made my peace. I hated how I looked, but I knew it was coming. I hated cutting my hair short, and the salon experience was heart-wrenching, but this was my reality. My son, Vihaan, didn't notice the first haircut. The second haircut was so much shorter that he noticed, but quickly went back to playing. When my hair fell out, Vihaan didn't care one bit. I could look like a toad, but my children still thought the world of me. I was their world, and my hair, or lack of it, wouldn't change that.

I don't mean to imply that hair matters to adults. One evening my friends Pallav and Aiswarya came over, and I was sick of wearing my hat. I said, "I hope it doesn't bother you that I'm not wearing the hat." And both vehemently told me it didn't matter one bit. And it really didn't to them. But as adults, I know we equate that sickly baldness with chemotherapy, and it can affect our perceptions of someone, even if only subconsciously. I was relieved that my children were so young that they were oblivious to my suffering and physical appearance. That is the beauty of unconditional love: it's pure.

It was comforting to me when Stephanie told me how beautiful I was or how pretty my eyes were. She didn't brush aside my baldness; she said that, if it were her, the loss of hair would be the most traumatic part of chemotherapy. So many people told me I looked beautiful, or that my baldness didn't even faze them. I appreciated that, but sometimes it was nice to hear a woman admit that hair loss is traumatic. I still have dreams that my hair is long again, pre-cancer length. And these dreams are far too visceral. I wake up with a notion that I have long, luscious locks again, only to come to terms with short, unruly curls. To accept that it will take years for me to look like myself again feels like a rude awakening.

It was a hard road, but I had the Master of Managing Chemotherapy Symptoms on my side. Stephanie is an extraordinary oncologist. She believed in being ahead of the game, ahead of pain, ahead of the nausea. Catching up is very hard, she explained. When something didn't work, she had an alternative. She answered my calls over the weekend, and would even apologize if she had missed a text or a voicemail. Her humanity left me humbled.

Cancer treatment is fairly uniform across the country, which is why doctors refer to a "standard of care." However, the management of symptoms is dependent on the expertise of the oncologist and the willingness of the patient to agree to and to follow a medication regimen. A fellow survivor told me that, during her treatment, her oncologist said that Taxol isn't very hard on the body, and the doctor didn't give her anti-nausea drugs preemptively. As a result, this sweet friend of mine was puking her guts out during treatment. I, on the other hand, went through seven cycles of chemotherapy without throwing up once, because Stephanie was such a whiz at managing symptoms.

I was initially cautious about texting Stephanie, thinking I should use this privilege in cases of urgency and desperation only. That lasted all of two weeks. Before long I was texting her the color of my eyeshadow or the name of the perfume I was wearing. Stephanie found me hilarious, I think. I told myself that wasn't hard to accomplish, given that her average patient was more than sixty-five years old. Moreover, I have a knack for clawing my way into people's hearts. Ask Degaulle.

The point is, Stephanie used every tool she had to help me get through chemotherapy. It was by no means a walk in the park, but I've heard of others who had it far worse. I was on twelve to fourteen pills a day, but that's what it took for me to get through chemo. It's imperative to remember there is no cookie-cutter treatment for cancer; moreover, there is no glory in suffering. Chemo creates havoc in the body. You ought to have an oncologist who will do everything he or she can to help keep the symptoms at bay.

The halfway point of chemotherapy was bittersweet. Of course Nuwan and I were happy that I was done with four cycles, but I was getting progressively more tired. With the cycles being two weeks apart, I did not have much time to recover from one session before it was time for more poison. The fatigue was cumulative, and it never actually got better, only worse. Having said that, I want to point out how proud my mother was of me when it came to handling chemotherapy. The steroids made me hungry, and I ate nutritious homecooked meals with an emphasis on protein. Such a voracious appetite meant I had energy, which was a good sign. Even though I needed naps and eleven to twelve hours of sleep every night, I had a lot of energy during the day—enough to go to work and enough to be a mother. Aai told me this was not the case for most of the chemotherapy patients she had seen. Though I was suffering, I was grateful for the small victories. Cancer picked the wrong girl to mess with.

My sister-in-law Priyanka visited from Dubai, leaving her five-month-old son behind with her husband, so that she could be with us at a critical juncture in my treatment. I was due to get an ultrasound to evaluate how the tumors were reacting to chemotherapy. When I was biopsied, you may remember, the radiologist inserted miniscule titanium markers into the tumors. These markers act as a scale to measure the tumor against (and for those lucky women whose biopsy results show no sign of cancer, the markers remain in the body for future mammograms).

We were in good spirits that day. Nuwan and I knew the results would be favorable, because by the third chemotherapy cycle, I couldn't feel my tumors anymore. I was confident the tumors had shrunk. Priyanka kept Nuwan company as we awaited the impending good news.

The ultrasound was tricky; it took the technician a few minutes of prodding to find the marker in the lymph node. But again, that was a good sign. Dr. Zusan looked at the ultrasound results and came in to talk to us. She did a physical exam and then gave us the good news: the tumors had shrunk by more than 75 percent! It was music to our ears. Priyanka had been praying the whole time I had the test. Priya was eagerly waiting for my call. Everyone was relieved; our prayers had been answered. I texted my cousins and called my aunts and uncles. There was a collective sigh of relief from all. Stephanie's chemotherapy cocktail was working.

Priyanka came to the cancer center with me for my fifth cycle. As they got me prepped and ready for the infusion, she broke down. She was so distraught, devastated that her little brother's wife was battling cancer. She cried and told me how brave I was. I know this was extremely difficult for her to see.

In the meantime, work remained a welcome diversion, and an opportunity came up for me to travel to Palo Alto, to collaborate with a human-centered design company. This was a unique opportunity that I did not want to miss out on. You might wonder, "Why bother? Just tell work that you have cancer and skip the travel." But you see, working with this consultancy was one of the highlights during chemotherapy. It gave me a creative distraction to focus my energy on. Traveling would be a huge show of strength for me and a slap in the face of chemotherapy. But I needed a porter and healthcare guardian to make this trip happen. I had Priyanka for this. Traveling to Palo Alto boosted my spirits.

And Priyanka's two-week visit made a world of a difference to Nuwan's spirits. It brought life and laughter into the house. She gave my mother company on the days that I wanted to rest, and she doted on her niece and nephew. To help Priyanka's husband Neil with childcare duties while she was with us, Neil's mother flew from Northern Ireland to Dubai. There is an undeniable sense of family in my clan. Even my sister-in-law's own in-laws knew how important it was for Nuwan to have his sister by his side.

When we started on Taxol during the fifth cycle of my chemotherapy, it triggered neuropathy. Stephanie had cautioned me about it. Neuropathy is temporary and often reversible nerve damage to your extremities. I couldn't feel the tips of my fingers, which made buttoning up my children's clothes impossible. The soles of my feet hurt a lot, too, especially in the morning. It was like being on pins and needles, but worse, because it shook my balance. Stephanie told us that if she continued to administer the same dosage of

Taxol the nerve damage would be irreversible. So she reduced the dosage
to make sure that, at the end of all this, I would retain my quality of life.
She is a gifted oncologist, who can look at the big picture.

• • •

At the start of chemotherapy, getting to the finish line seemed
excruciatingly long. Stephanie decided to stop my chemotherapy
with cycle seven and not to give me cycle eight at all, a careful
decision she made based on the effects Taxol was having on my body, and
on how much the tumors had shrunk with four cycles. It came as a big
surprise when Nuwan and I went in for cycle seven, and Stephanie said
this would be my last chemotherapy appointment! It seemed unreal. Just
like that, three and half months of hell, and it's over already? I breathed
a huge sigh of relief. I had kicked chemo's butt.

I'll admit that the feeling of elation was short-lived as anxiety set in for
what was coming next. I was a month away from my double mastectomy.
But I wanted to conclude my chemo experience on a positive note. I
handwrote twelve thank you cards for the oncology nurses who cared for
me and dropped off muffins and treats for them. I also got a small gift for
Stephanie and wrote her the following letter:

Dear Stephanie,

During the darkest time of my life you gave us hope. Your
oncology knowledge and ability to manage the nastiest of
symptoms made my chemo surmountable. Your wicked sense
of humor and sarcasm helped us come to grips with my new
reality while sharing a hearty laugh.

THANK YOU for always checking in on me and calling
in prescriptions over the weekend. I am humbled by your
medical prowess and your empathy. I love your brutal honesty

and I thank you from the bottom of my heart.

From,

Your favorite 35-year-old Indian cancer patient Niyati
Tamaskar & her stoic British Sri Lankan hubby Nuwan.

• • •

In the early stages of my diagnosis, when I made my cancer public
knowledge, my manager informed me of a service my company
provides during medical emergencies called Advanced Medical.
This program gives employees a chance to request a second opinion.
Not just any second opinion, but one from top-notch medical experts
in the field. All I needed to do was to electronically sign a release form
for my medical information. After the Advanced Medical team had the
information, they would then consult with the country's best physicians
to generate a detailed treatment plan for me. I found a link to the service
and provided an e-signature, which set the wheels in motion for Harvard
Medical School and Massachusetts General Hospital in Boston to review
my files.

Within a matter of days I was contacted by Dr. Kerry Reynolds, oncology
director at Massachusetts General. This brilliant woman has one of the
kindest voices I've ever heard. She genuinely cared about my situation
and spent a lot of time explaining my cancer to me. In the early stages of
my diagnosis, when the staging of my cancer was uncertain, I spoke to
her about my fears of being Stage 4. Dr. Reynolds reassured me that even
at Stage 4, there were several treatment options, and that life expectancy
for cancer had changed dramatically in recent years. What I liked about
her was that she didn't feed me some horseshit, like, "Don't worry, it
won't be Stage 4." Because guess what: everything in my life was now
uncertain. Dr. Reynolds was in touch with me through many steps of my
treatment and patiently answered several questions.

I also received a report generated by a team of physicians from Harvard Medical School. They were in agreement with the treatment plan that Stephanie had laid out for me. They had a lot of statistics attached to the report and an appendix with references. Stephanie and Vikram were both impressed by the thoroughness of the document.

I feel blessed to work for a company that offers a service like Advanced Medical. It shows that the company cares about its employees. I thank God for putting me in this country, where I had the best possible chance of survival. I thank God for giving me Nuwan, without whom this fight would have been impossible. And I thank God for my children. For them I vowed to fight like a tigress.

• • •

Before the mastectomy, there was still an important piece of the puzzle we needed to sort out regarding breast reconstruction. You're thinking, *Oh, a boob job?* Wrong. Breast reconstruction is complicated, because there is no breast tissue left. It is building boobs from nothing. It requires the work of a plastic surgeon, and with Degaulle's recommendation, we added Dr. Jackson to Team Tamaskar.

Our first meeting with Dr. Jackson was tough. He explained the process of reconstruction, and it sounded barbaric. After the breast surgeon finishes the mastectomy, he said, he would go in and place tissue expanders behind the pectoral muscle. He had a sample of a tissue expander that he showed us. It is a balloon-like structure with a plastic port, which provides an access to add or remove saline. Dr. Jackson told us that he would inject the expanders with small amounts of saline, 25 cc at a time, to eventually create a cavity in the chest. Once the expansion was complete, I would need another surgery to insert silicone implants, and the tissue expanders would be removed. I asked him if the expanders were painful. He said that initially they are, because it's like a bulldozer creating space. But women get used to the pain, he said, adding that it feels like when a mother has "let down" during breastfeeding.

He saw the worried faces Nuwan and I made. He looked at me and said, "I don't know what it's like being in your shoes, but…", and then he looked at Nuwan, "my wife had breast cancer, so I know what it's like to be on that side of the table." He assured us that I would do better than I thought, and we were going to be okay. Dr. Jackson was so kindhearted. Degaulle for another win! His recommendation panned out yet again.

My case was complicated, said Dr. Jackson. "Because of the radiation therapy you will receive after surgery, we need to wait six months before I can replace the expanders with silicone implants." Six months of this barbaric tissue expander in my body? This would extend the timeline out to 2019. I wanted to be done in 2018. I needed to be done this year. I had a goal, and the finish line for it was December 2018. Dr. Jackson left the room, and I started crying. Nuwan consoled me. "A few more months, honey, only a few more months. We can do this together."

While we were sitting there, Dr. Jackson came back in to tell us something. He noticed the waterworks and said, "If your eyes have been watering lately, it's a common side effect of Taxol. Ask Dr. Wagner to prescribe you something for it."

"Dr. Jackson, these are tears," I said.

He didn't understand why I was upset. I explained to him the mental preparation that it had required to get to this point, as well as my hope that my cancer treatment would wrap up in 2018. But now that timeline had been blown out of the water. It was "a side effect of chemotherapy," he said. Men are so clueless.

7. KILLER BOOBS

**"Sometimes we love with nothing more than hope.
Sometimes we cry with everything except tears."**
— Gregory David Roberts, *Shantaram*

I had four weeks to mentally and physically prepare for surgery. Nothing can prepare you for a double mastectomy, however. I just want to establish that. I don't care what you've heard, which support group you've attended, what church you visit, or how many gods you pray to. It doesn't matter if you see a therapist or meditate every morning. Nothing can prepare a woman for losing one of the most essential parts of her femininity. My hair was long gone, but I still had my breasts. I was still a woman. Losing my breasts has been the hardest thing I've had to endure. Harder than chemo and its toxic cocktails.

I wanted to get into shape for the surgery. I went a bit crazy and started going to the gym five times a week. I was working out and active, pushing my body to its brink, post-chemotherapy. During that time, I made friends with women at the gym. It's hard to overlook a bald, bloated, hunchbacked, moon-faced chemotherapy patient. My new gym buddies were kind to me; they said they would pray for me and wished me well during surgery. I also found myself a new support group. On June 25, I turned thirty-five. I went to the gym, as I did every morning. Before the PiYo (Pilates and yoga) session started I said to the instructor and the class, "Tracy, it's my thirty-fifth birthday today! I might be bald but I'm kicking ass." Everyone laughed and wished me a happy birthday.

I called Vikram *dada* often, more than I'd like to admit. He was my support system. More often than not I was distraught. It is really hard for me to say this out loud, or to write it: *I was scared.* They were going to surgically remove my breasts. I wasn't afraid of the surgery or the pain. I was scared about waking up after surgery. I told Vikram, "Dada, I wish I didn't have to wake up from the surgery." I was in mourning. Some might describe my state of mind as that of a depressed person. But let's get real—this was a calamity. And if cancer isn't going to cause some amount of depression and anxiety, then what else would?

I allowed myself to be upset about losing my identity as a woman, even though that's not what most people wanted to hear or see. I was bombarded with messages about staying strong and being positive. So here's me, a cancer survivor and mother, telling you that sometimes you get dealt a crappy hand. And in those times, it's okay to say, "This stinks!" (In fact, feel free to add expletives to that sentence and to acknowledge your feelings.)

Life went on. No matter how many times I called Vikram *dada* crying, I was still a mother to my children. I played with them, laughed with them, loved them, and held them close. I still went to work and functioned as a high-performing engineer. My only regret is that I never said this out loud: "They're not *just boobs.* They're an integral part of my identity."

There was a popular misconception floating around during my cancer treatment. Several friends, family members, and even physicians we knew insisted that, "Chemotherapy is the worst of it. Surgery will be a lot easier." Chemotherapy is devastating, true, but how could anyone think that surgery would be easier? It baffled me. To wake up without breasts—how does one cope with that? I thought about it long and hard and came up with this reasoning: chemotherapy is in your face. It is the bald patient throwing up and sleeping for hours. It is hard to ignore, and you cannot look away. Surgery is under my shirt. It is silent and not in anyone's face. To the outside world, watching their loved ones battle cancer, chemotherapy is all too visceral. But surgery is hidden. I didn't know much about what I was going to experience post-surgery, but even then I knew a mastectomy must be traumatic. How could it not be?

I worked throughout my entire chemotherapy, finally taking disability leave before my surgery. On my last day at work we had a project review scheduled, with participation from key managers. A colleague, Tom, asked me if I was all right with him doing a little thank you speech for me for working with this team. I was fine with it. Tom kicked off the meeting with introductions, made a speech thanking me for being an inspiration and working during chemotherapy, and then wished me luck with the rest of the treatment. Another colleague, Becca, had organized a care package for me with a blanket, some warm socks, lotions, Chapstick, and nail polish. It was so thoughtful. They also had a card in there with messages from the entire team. I was so touched. I wanted to use this opportunity to thank the whole team, so I typed up a speech during the five-minute coffee break and practiced it in my head. Here's how it went:

> I would like to take this opportunity to thank the Zenith and
> Tag teams. In March, while I was in the middle of workshops
> with Tom and Maggie, and finalizing the HCD proposal
> with Allison, I was diagnosed with Stage 3 breast cancer. My
> husband Nuwan Gallege and I were shell-shocked, but very
> quickly, we needed to make a plan on how to get through this.
>
> Here's where all of you come in. Zenith and Tag team gave
> me the motivation to stay focused on work. Cancer started to
> claim parts of me—my hair, my dreams . . . well, nightmares,

hours of my day—while I bounced between doctor
consultations. But you know what cancer couldn't take away?
My work and my desire to do meaningful work. So, I did just
that. I worked through seven cycles of chemotherapy. Having
my laptop open, responding to email or working on slides
and even calling in to meetings while at the hospital during
chemotherapy infusions, kept me strong. Going to Palo Alto
was a huge show of strength and a personal win.

I stand here before you, follically challenged but eternally
grateful to each and every one of you for helping me in this
journey. Tom and Becca, it has been an honor to work with
you. Thank you.

I choked up when I made this speech. It was the first time I had stood in
front of a crowd saying, "I have breast cancer" out loud. Some colleagues
were in tears while I spoke. After the project review was done, and it was
time for me to head home, everyone gave me hugs. The unlikeliest of
people, the introverts and engineers, gave me hugs. I was told that I was
a true inspiration, I was told to keep the group informed of my progress,
and I was wished luck. People said they would pray for me. I will cherish
the memory of that meeting forever.

• • •

So many things in life can be simplified if you have a workplace that
is supportive and compassionate. And that starts at the first level
up, your manager. I was blessed to be working for a gentleman
named John, who had seen a loved one battle cancer and felt deep
sympathy for my situation. It doesn't matter if a group president gives
you a pep talk, or executive leadership drops food off at your doorstep, if
your direct manager is a hard taskmaster. Having John, my first line of
defense, on my side, emphasizing the importance of my battle over the
nuances of work, empowered me. You might assume here that John and

I had a long-term working relationship, that he knew me pre-cancer, but that's incorrect. John became a manager to my team a few days after my diagnosis. I'm sure he was thrilled: "Here's your new team. Oh, and one of them is battling cancer." (That's British sarcasm for you.)

Nobody likes to deal with personnel issues, and among them grave health woes are probably the least favorite. But John didn't shy away from the situation. He got personal and wanted to find ways to help me. The first time John and I met face-to-face was the first day I wore my wig and stepped out of the house. As I walked into the conference room, I started to shake nervously, because I felt like an imposter. And John noticed that. I told him later why I was shaking, that I felt like a phony. He sent me a link to some awesome chemotherapy hats. He encouraged me to do whatever made me feel like myself and what was comfortable: wear a wig, wear a hat, or let the baldness shine. When I hear about friends with needlessly tough bosses, micromanaging managers, and clock-watching supervisors, I feel terrible. Because those things do not improve productivity, nor do they create an environment conducive to innovation. Show your employees empathy and compassion, and you will win their loyalty. John certainly won mine.

• • •

The night before my surgery, July 11, 2018, Vikram drove three hours from Ohio to be with us. We ate and stayed up till 11:30 p.m., so that I could eat another snack before bed. I had been told not to consume water or food after midnight, and I wanted to make sure that I wouldn't go hungry. My surgery wasn't until noon the next day, but they wanted me at the hospital for pre-surgical procedures at 10 a.m. Vikram, Priya, Nuwan, and I dropped the kids off at daycare and headed to Community Hospital in Greenwood for my surgery. Vikram and Priya drove separately so they could drive back as needed to help with the kids. About twenty minutes into the drive I teared up. Nuwan started crying as he was driving. He said he couldn't believe this was happening to us. I was in tears, still in disbelief. *How is this happening to us? What did I do wrong? Nuwan doesn't deserve this.*

When we got to the hospital all tears were wiped away and emotions set aside. Vikram, Priya, Nuwan, and I chatted and laughed. It was time for me to check into my room. As we all sat in there a nurse came in to say that the anesthesiologist was on his way. I asked if it was Dr. Payne. She said, "No, it's Dr. Strain." You can't make this stuff up! The alternative to Dr. Payne was Dr. Strain. *Are you kidding me? Does Community Hospital only hire anesthesiologists with rhyming names?* I missed Dr. Payne and his impeccable bedside manner.

We heard a knock on the door, and there it was, a familiar face: Dr. Payne! I was so relieved, but I had to use this opportunity to give him a hard time. "Dr. Payne, I thought I was going to get Dr. Strain. So, what's the deal with the anesthesiology department? You only hire people with rhyming names?" He laughed. We exchanged more quips, and then I asked him to repeat my request about my glasses: don't take them off too soon, and be sure to put them back on before I'm awake. He said he remembered.

Before surgery they wanted to inject a dye into my areola and wait to see how it would drain from the breast to the lymph nodes. This meant getting three shots around my nipple while I was awake and not numbed. It was painful, and this was before surgery had even started. How bad was surgery going to be? I shuddered at the thought. After the dye injection I went back to the pre-op room. It was time for them to roll me away. Before leaving I told Nuwan, "Honey, I have a letter for you and Priya. It's in the suitcase. Please read that while I'm in surgery." Then I turned to Vikram and said, "Dada, I'm sorry I didn't write you a letter." And then to all three of them, "I love you."

I kissed my husband and was rolled away. It was one of the saddest moments of my life. To be rolled away from my husband with my breasts for the last time. After this I would have no breasts.

I got to the operating room, and there was Dr. Zusan. She introduced me to the nurses in the room. The nurses asked me to move onto the operating table, and I followed their instructions. I got on the table, removed my glasses, handed them over, saw Dr. Zusan, then burst out crying. I covered my face with my hands and said, "This is the last time I am going to have my breasts. What did I do wrong, Dr. Zusan? How is this happening to me?" I said a few more things that I don't recall and cried profusely for a few minutes. We didn't have all day for feelings, though—it was time for surgery. Dr. Zusan offered encouraging words to me. Dr. Payne, on the other hand, was clueless, and said, "I think she wants her glasses." I thought to myself, *I really ought to get Dr. Payne and Dr. Jackson in a room to talk about emotions.* This made me chuckle to myself. Humor helped my brain to cope, even just moments before major surgery. It was a relief valve in such a high-stress environment.

I was ready. I lay down; no one rushed me. The anesthesia was administered, and within seconds I was asleep. This is the last memory I have of my breasts.

On July 12, 2018, probably around 1 p.m., at the age of thirty-five, I lost my breasts to cancer. One was cancerous, and the other was removed prophylactically. As we had discussed, Dr. Jackson reconstructed my breasts and put tissue expanders on each side.

• • •

Approximately five and a half hours later I woke up, groggy and in excruciating pain. I made eye contact with Nuwan, Vikram, and Priya. I told Nuwan that I wanted to hold Vikram's hand, and he immediately reached out. It was the saddest moment of my life.

Not because I lost my breasts, but because I woke up without them. The whole time I was secretly hoping I would not wake up. This way I could say I fought the disease, but I wouldn't have to deal with the aftermath. I wanted to stay asleep forever—but I didn't, which meant I had to continue fighting.

The first night after surgery was hell on earth. To put it bluntly, the on-call nurse was a heartless bitch. I apologize for the cursing; I suppose I should give her the benefit of doubt. Maybe she had a bad day, or got a flat tire, or maybe her dishwasher broke. But maybe she should've given me the benefit of compassion. I had just gone through a double mastectomy and a dissection of multiple lymph nodes. What did the nurse who-shall-never-be-named do? She didn't believe me when I told her the level of pain I was in. When she assessed my pain level the evening after the surgery, I told her my pain was a 7 on a scale from 1–10. She gave me mild narcotics. An hour later I pressed the button to have her check on me. When she arrived I told her my pain was an "8".

"You were at 7, and I gave you medicine, and now you're at 8?" she asked, suspiciously.

"Yes, the medicine wore off, and I'm in tremendous pain from the double mastectomy: the drain site hurts, my chest hurts. It's excruciating."

She just stared. I thought maybe if I gave her some context she would get a better sense of where I was coming from. "I want you know that when I was in labor, during contractions, at 7 centimeters dilated, when I was asked about pain, I told them I was at 6. Before the epidural, at 7 centimeters, I was a 6! I want you to know how painful this is, and that I have been through labor and know how bad that is."

Instead of taking my word for it and helping me, she said, "I know women with third-degree tears that don't rate their pain at a 7." I was appalled.

She should've listened to me. But she refused to give me medication to help with the pain. When I asked her if there was a doctor on call, she said, "There's always a doctor on call," and then stormed out of the room.

And so I was left alone with my pain. I called my cousin Vikrant, an ER doctor on the West Coast, and told him about the situation. He was enraged and asked to speak to the imbecile. He was stern with her and told her there was no need for me to be in pain *at all*, and that it was her duty to help me post-surgery in any way she could. The nurse came back to my room and administered more drugs. She was in a foul mood and was incredibly rude to me. I still thanked her for her help, because I wanted to be the bigger person. In hindsight I should have sued the hospital and gotten her fired. A person who cannot be kind to a cancer patient who just lost both breasts should not be in the medical field—or any field that involves human, animal, or plant interaction.

After the worst night possible I was eager to get home, where we could take charge of managing my pain without judgment. On our way out Nuwan and I voiced our grievances to the hospital staff, who profusely apologized on the hospital's behalf and ensured me that corrective actions would be taken. (A pre-cancer Niyati would've followed up to make sure they were.)

At home we were greeted by my loving niece Arya, Vikram, Beena, and Priya. It was all-hands-on-deck to help out post-surgery and to keep the children entertained and happy. We had so much support, morally and physically, that it made this ordeal bearable. Seeing the children upset would've crushed my soul. Priya engulfed Aarini with so much love that I'm certain she thought *Priya* was her mom. Beena took over the kitchen and played with Vihaan, and Arya doted on both kids. Having a house full of the people to whom I was closest made this battle surmountable. I shudder to think of people going through this ordeal alone. How do they get help? Those are the true warriors. Not me; I asked for help. I made

speeches, wrote letters, texted, emailed, called, and cried. I wince when I
hear of people hiding their disease.

I had been discharged from the hospital with two drains sticking out of
my sides, a rubber tube, and a little reservoir to collect lymphatic fluid.
Nuwan emptied the drains for me multiple times a day, and we recorded
the amount of fluid collected. With the drains in my body I was told not
to use my arms for anything more than eating and brushing my teeth.
Rest assured, doctors, this wasn't an issue: I was in so much pain that
Priya had to feed me. It hurt to move my arms, and my chest wall hurt
too.

During the double mastectomy the surgeon took off the top layer of
muscle from the pectoral muscles, which affected my upper-body strength
and range of motion. Losing lymph nodes was hard on my body too.
But the emotional pain was just as hard. It was incredibly challenging to
refrain from picking up my baby girl. Vihaan would come lay by my feet
and touch me gently. I was able to give him some amount of physical
affection, but I just couldn't do the same for my daughter. During this
time Priya became an interim mother for Aarini. She did everything for
her and Vihaan.

The right drain was removed on day six, and it was such a relief. But the
left drain—on the side that was missing seven lymph nodes—stayed in
for twenty days. That took a toll on my recovery. The weeks following
the surgery were arduous. I marveled at the human ability to tolerate
pain and endure. I slept a lot. I felt like I had been hit by a train. I was so
fatigued that I thought there must be something wrong with me. I asked
the physicians who took care of me, and Vikram, about this. All of them
assured me this was a good sign, that the body needs rest to rebuild itself.
I had to be reminded of human biology, that sleep is when the body heals.
I gave in, and I rested.

My cousin Deepak's wife Suzanne came from Chicago, leaving their five-year-old daughter with Deepak to help post-surgery. (Remember the male ban?) It was a welcome visit. She spoiled Vihaan and Aarini rotten and gave me time to recuperate.

On July 20, a Friday evening, I got a call from the hospital. Priya, Nuwan, and Apurva were all there, but I stepped into the bedroom to hear what they had to say by myself. I knew the call was to inform me about the pathology of the breasts and lymph nodes. Dr. Zusan had told me there was a two-step process to finding out if chemotherapy worked. The first step was done during surgery, while I was on the operating table. The lymph nodes that were dissected got checked in an on-site laboratory. If any of them had turned up positive for cancer, Dr. Zusan would have removed all the remaining lymph nodes from my left armpit. Fortunately, the lymph nodes tested negative. Even though I lost seven, Dr. Zusan did not need to remove "the fatty pad," as she called it.

The second step of the confirmation process was to send my breast mass and lymph nodes for further screening after surgery. According to Dr. Zusan, the breast tissue would be dissected in 2-mm sections and checked for any live cancer cells. The results take approximately two weeks to get back. If all the tissue was negative it would mean I had a "pathologic complete response." This is a great indicator of survival and is the best-case scenario. If the lymph nodes had any sign of cancer I would have to go back in for more surgery, and Dr. Zusan would need to remove all my lymph nodes from the left side. It would mean that chemotherapy didn't kill all the cancer cells.

This was the call I had been waiting for and dreading. My heart was pounding out of my chest.

The nurse sounded somber, which I thought wasn't a good sign. "Hi, Ms. Tamaskar. I have the pathology results from your surgery. The left breast tissue is negative for cancer. We also tested the right breast, and it was negative for cancer . . ."

There it was. I was anticipating a *"but"*, since she didn't sound positive from the get-go. "We tested seven lymph nodes, and all seven tested 'negative' for cancer," she added. I couldn't believe what she had just told me. I didn't run into the living room, and I didn't share the news with anyone. Instead I asked her, "I'm sorry, what? Does this mean that I've had a pathologic complete response?" She finally cracked a smile, I could tell from her voice, and said, "Yes, Ms. Tamaskar, everything was negative for cancer. You have had a pathologic complete response. PCR."

I thanked her profusely for calling on a Friday and giving us such good news. I hung up and ran to the living room. "Honey, Priya, Apu, I just got a call from the nurse and she had my test results. I am CANCER-FREE! I've had a pathologic complete response, no live cancer cells, everything was negative for cancer. Both breasts and all seven lymph nodes, negative for cancer!" The word "negative" had never sounded this positive. I'm not sure it ever will again.

Nuwan ran to me. He picked me up and kissed me, and we hugged. Priya and Apurva were hugging. I hugged my sister, and my cousin was in tears. We were so happy. And then a shadow of doubt crept over me. I was the only one who heard the nurse; what if I was wrong? What if I misheard? *Is this really happening?* I decided to call the nurse navigator at Dr. Zusan's office to reconfirm the results. Sarah picked up the phone, and I asked her if she had access to my results. She said she did and sounded happy. "Sarah, I'm putting you on speaker. I have my family gathered around the phone; can you please read out the results and confirm the news? I am in disbelief. We are all so happy. But please repeat this for my sake." She graciously obliged and reread the results on speaker so everyone could hear. Sarah told us I had a PCR, a pathologic complete response, to chemotherapy.

It was official, but I wasn't done yet. I wanted to see the results with my own eyes. I knew just the man who would help me do so, someone who would have access to my files. Degaulle, of course. As Nuwan got the champagne out, I ran next door. I needed to see this. Degaulle, bless his heart, was resting on the couch, probably back from a forty-eight-hour shift delivering screaming babies to screaming mothers. I'm sure all he wanted was some peace. Well, too bad! He opened the door. I hugged him, then said, "Degaulle, I just found out I am cancer-free, I've had a PCR." He knew the acronym; I didn't need to say more. He was so happy and relieved for me.

"Come on in. Let's take a look." He pulled up his laptop and within seconds was able to access my file. He read it out to me, showing me what it said and confirming everything we had just heard. There was no denying it: the killer boobs had been amputated, I had had a complete response to chemotherapy, and I was cancer-free. Praise Krishna.

8. GENTLE HEALING BEAM

**"I talked and he listened, drawing the shame from me
like a healer draws infection from a wound."**
— Tara Westover, *Educated*

The joy of breaking the news about my PCR to friends and family was unparalleled. A special incident that sticks out in my mind is when I told Suma, a friend in Seattle, about it. She was at a quarterly staff meeting when she saw my note. Suma told me that, at the meeting, colleagues go around the table and say one thing they are thankful for. Suma went first. She told her colleagues that, "My dear friend, after a very tough battle, has been diagnosed to be cancer-free." Upon hearing this, her workmates unanimously decided this would be their highlight, too, because nothing could top it. The thought of strangers celebrating with me, for me, was empowering. I was so touched by that. There is so much goodness in this world. (It is my sincere hope that you feel the same way after reading this book, that there is hope for humanity.)

After the merriment of having a pathologic complete response to chemotherapy, reality stared us back in the face again in the form of lymphedema. Lymphedema is the swelling of the arms that results from damage to or removal of lymph nodes. I spent a few weeks in rehabilitation to treat it. This was done on an outpatient basis. The therapist taught me low-intensity arm and shoulder exercises that I needed to do at home every day. The highlight of my appointments was the lymphedema massage she would give. Although painful, it felt like I was receiving the cancer-spa treatment. The aim was to get me to where I could lift my left arm above my head, which I'd have to do in order to start radiation.

During this time I was still bargaining in my head. *Would I really need six and a half weeks of radiation, Monday through Friday?* Maybe they will go easy on the radiation; maybe I would just need half the dose. But that was wishful thinking. Based on Degaulle's recommendation we reached out to Dr. McMullen to be our radiation oncologist. A long conversation with him made it quite clear that I needed the whole dose. Radiation was the last step of my treatment, and it was just as important as all the previous ones. Seven cycles of chemotherapy followed by a double mastectomy and lymph node dissection and radiation to finish up the grueling schedule.

Dr. McMullen is, for lack of a better word, special. Our first session with him lasted approximately two hours. Dr. McMullen thoroughly answered our questions, stepped away for a few minutes to perform a stereotactic procedure, came back, and then continued to answer our questions. There was no doubt in my mind that Nuwan and I were in good hands. He talked about survivorship, and how life after a cancer journey is often unrecognizable, and that it takes patients some time to get used to the new normal. He said he would work hard to minimize radiation damage to the lungs and heart. I felt at ease when he told us about the time he spent in pediatric oncology. He cared about the long-term effects of radiation and quality of life. That was the serious side of him, but it didn't take too long for us to connect on a more intimate level. I quickly discovered that he is hilarious—part genius and part bonkers, a perfect blend. His heart is magnanimous and his soul genuine. He called radiation "the gentle healing beam," to which Nuwan added, "You mean the DNA-altering, gentle healing beam?"

Dr. McMullen had the impossible job of explaining radiation treatment to us, and he rose to the occasion. Since I had left-sided breast cancer, he explained, he needed the right side to remain flat or fairly flat, so he could get the angles he needed without damaging my heart. As a consequence, once my drains were out Dr. Jackson injected small amounts of saline into the left breast tissue expander but kept the right one flat.

The expanders made my breast rock-hard, and the expansion process was extremely painful. The left side was expanded over five weeks, and since Dr. McMullen wanted the right side flat, I officially had a "uniboob". Beauty aside, I felt subhuman, deformed. I had two choices: accept my temporary uniboob status or hide. I say if you got it, flaunt it. I wore comfortable t-shirts, some fitted, others loose, some with V-necks. I had a long way to go to accept my new body. I'm still not there, and I don't know how I'll get there. But something Degaulle said to me helped: "If anyone could rock a uniboob it is you. You make it a fashion statement." Degaulle often told me he liked me bald, that I could pull it off with so much style. Now that my hair is growing back, he tells me I look great with short hair. At the risk of sounding vain I will admit that I need those affirmations.

A few weeks into the expansion process, Dr. Jackson asked me if I was satisfied with the size of the reconstructed areas. I looked in dismay, and asked, "What is this, a B-cup?" He said yes. I told him, "Dr. Jackson, before kids I was a 28DD. After kids I was a 32E. This mediocre B-cup isn't going to cut it." Without so much as flinching, he asked me to come back the following week for further expansion. As he was walking out the door he had his Dictaphone out. "Patient was a double-D . . ." he said, recording our discussion. I'm not embarrassed. I had had an amazing rack. Petite as I might be, my killer boobs were spectacular. I deserved to have some semblance of the old me. The oddest thing about the double mastectomy was the feeling of disassociation I had, and I still have, with my reconstructed breasts. I don't feel like they are a part of my body, because they look foreign to me. Also, the numbness bothers me a lot.

By the time I got to radiation, I was spent, emotionally and physically drained. The first couple of times that I spoke to Dr. McMullen, I was all joke-joke-laugh-laugh, at the top of my game. Fence off the heart, suppress vulnerability, and use humor as my shield. But that quickly faded, and soon enough Dr. McMullen saw me at my worst. I cried at the start of radiation, because I couldn't get my head around how this could have happened to me. I know you're probably thinking, *What? At the end of your treatment you're wondering how you got there?* But that's the thing with reality and emotions: you can put up a brave front, but it may all come crumbling down at any time. We are taught to be brave in the face of danger, but at some point, it'll get to you. Radiation is what got to me.

I cried during radiation simulations. This was meant to mimic what the procedure would be like, so I would be prepared for the real deal. They had me take my shirt off, exposing my scars. I lay still in the CT scan machine and performed as they asked me to. "Take a deep breath in and hold it," I was instructed. Dr. McMullen was using the breath-hold technique because he wanted my lungs full of air, pushing my heart as far away as possible from the radiation beam. After I broke down during the simulation, I asked to meet privately with Dr. McMullen, even though it wasn't planned. He was considerate and understood why I needed a consult.

I got past the simulations, but then it was time to start the actual treatment. Unlike the joy I felt when we started chemotherapy—and let me repeat, both Nuwan and I were THRILLED when I started my first session—radiation was dreadful. Dreadful because it caught me at my most vulnerable. Dreadful because I was so tired. My body had been through enough, only to get started with six and a half weeks of radiation therapy. Every. Single. Weekday.

The first session was as awful as I feared. I lay on a metal table for over an hour trying to master the breath-hold technique. The radiation therapists repositioned me for being millimeters off. They wrote on me with a permanent marker and taped over it so it would not rub off in the shower. I was inked! They promised me the following sessions would be better, and that the first one is the hardest. But the second round of radiation was no better. Dr. McMullen wasn't around that day, and it took almost two hours to get me in the correct position for a mere few minutes of radiation dosage. I wept after the second round because, even with all the lasers and infrared light, and the makeshift tattoos on my chest, the breath-hold technique just seemed unrepeatable. And I felt like I was failing. The radiation therapists would keep repositioning me. That's how hard they worked at protecting my lungs and heart. But still I lay there, on a hard metal table, without a shirt on, in a cold room, holding my breath for twenty seconds at a time, by myself, as they took x-ray images to ensure the beam would go to the exact location they wanted.

One of the worst parts about having cancer is how physically alone you are. I was alone at the mammogram, ultrasound, biopsy, MRI, PET scan, surgeries, radiation simulation, and radiation treatments. Nuwan was always around, but I was alone. Alone because he was far away in a waiting room, not allowed to be by my side. I would often text Stephanie saying, "I miss chemotherapy." Chemotherapy is a consistent, dependable poison. And Nuwan could be next to me; I could touch him, look at him, and it made me feel safe. Radiation though, was erratic, and, as an engineer, it frustrated me that the process was impossible to replicate. During one of my consults with Dr. McMullen, Nuwan and I were talking about all the tattoos I had on my skin that were used to help position me. Dr. McMullen said something like, "… and sometimes Niyati isn't perfectly lying there." I stopped him dead in his tracks.

"Dr. McMullen, I am perfect. It's *your* process that's irrational."

He started laughing and said, "Let's just stop here. We have established you are perfect. Just perfect." Humor to the rescue.

As I said, Dr. McMullen saw me at my worst. It was inevitable; radiation was relentless and exhausting. He let me cry, and he was kindhearted. I would always apologize, saying this wasn't the real me, that I was normally a much happier person. I told him that I had a wicked sense of humor. Dr. McMullen told me that he had no expectation of what I should be. He did not need to see an eternal optimist, jokester, or stand-up comedian. He was there for whatever I needed. If I was upset that day, then so be it. He allowed me to emote. That went against every grain in my body. I always thought a true hero is someone who endures and doesn't shed a tear. Vulnerability made me cringe. It was completely out of my comfort zone.

• • •

By this point you're probably thinking, *This book has a lot of tears and meltdowns: crying at the OB's office, the diagnosis, the breast surgeon—she is all tears!* You see, I'm letting you into the deepest, darkest secrets of my life. I am putting it all out there with only one agenda: human connection. I want to be relatable. And I'll admit that this sure beats going to therapy! I want my readers to know that they are not alone. You don't have to be a cancer survivor, or even a mother. Anyone going through a challenge can relate to my experiences. And everyone has challenges: demanding in-laws, an unforgiving boss, a cheating spouse, miscarriages, or a loved one battling cancer. I feel that the more connected the world has become, the more disconnected we are from each other. Texting and instant messaging is so convenient that people seldom talk on the phone. Social media enables us to share our story with the world, but it has become a rat race of showcasing "my fabulous life." In a world that is becoming increasingly sanctimonious and demands incessant optimism, this book is my attempt to stay grounded. It's a story of struggle, where fear is an acceptable emotion, vulnerability is a sign of courage, and staying positive is not a mandate.

At any rate, back to radiation. The moments of vulnerability were often overshadowed by the laughter I shared with others. For starters, I befriended the radiation therapists. One of them was recently divorced, and we talked about the dating scene. I gave another one a hard time about not proposing to his long-term girlfriend. The more I learned about Dr. McMullen, the more ammunition I had on him. "Friendly banter", as I like to call it. During one of my last radiation sessions, Dr. McMullen walked into the radiation therapy room in the middle of my repositioning. I asked him, "Dr. McMullen, are you lost?" He had never come into the room during treatment before. He said he wanted to have a word with me. One of the therapists, who is sweet as candy, kicked him out, explaining that we were in the middle of radiation. And I backed her up. "Dr. McMullen, do you have any idea how hard the breath-hold technique is? I am getting repositioned for being 3 mm off. Who in the world made these radiation plans that are impossible to replicate?" All the radiation therapists laughed; the plans are made by Dr. McMullen and his team, of course. Then he made the mistake of saying, "No, I thought you were done, because they were helping you up."

"I beg your pardon? *They* were helping me up? Do I look like an invalid? What, because I have cancer, you don't think I can get up on my own?"

He knew at that point there was nothing he could say. He apologized, and as everyone laughed, he left the therapy room. Walking into MY radiation session unannounced—*pssh*.

When Dr. McMullen wanted a word with me, I didn't think much of it. He always wanted a word with his favorite patient, I figured. When I visited him after the session ended, he introduced me to a friend who was going through breast cancer treatment. I wanted to give him a hard time in front of his friend, so I started by saying, "Well, Stephanie told me to call her by her first name the day we met. And you still insist on me calling you Dr. McMullen." He was emphatic when he claimed, "I've always asked you to call me Kevin. Call me Kevin." Apocryphal! ("Apocryphal" means something that is fictitious, a fun word I learned from watching the Mr. Peabody & Sherman movie with my four-year-old. I'm not being an Erudite Leader here, I swear.) I'm certain that Dr. McMullen had never asked me to call him Kevin. But now that he finally had, I would henceforth refer to him as Kevin.

Kevin then got to the bottom of this meeting. He was working on a plan to administer three additional doses of radiation to my internal mammary lymph nodes. The lymph nodes showed up as positive on the PET scan, but there was no way to do a biopsy to confirm if they were cancerous, because they are located behind the sternum. Kevin had consulted with four radiation oncologists from top cancer centers on the East Coast to get more opinions. Their vote was split 50–50. Two of them said I didn't need additional *rads* (radiation doses), because I had had a complete response to chemotherapy. The other two said it would be better to be cautious and give me the additional doses because of my young age, the aggressive nature of the tumor, and the minimal data there is on positive mammary lymph nodes. Kevin asked me what I wanted to do. It was a no-brainer for me: more radiation, of course.

But I wasn't going to make it easy for Kevin. I asked a few questions; I always ask questions. Question 1: Who were these experts he consulted with? He said he couldn't tell me, because this was off the record, as is common practice among oncologists. Question 2: What were the short- and long-term side effects of additional radiation? These were no different than the side-effects from the first twenty-five sessions of radiation. Question 3: Well, this was really more of a demand than a question. I told Kevin he needed to talk to Nuwan and explain the plan, since he wasn't here with me, and I didn't want to be responsible for making such crucial medical decisions on my own. Nuwan talked to Kevin on the phone, and he gave his consent. He asked how I was doing with the news, and if I felt comfortable. Kevin assured him I was all right.

At least, that's how it went down from my perspective. Nuwan's version of this story is slightly more comical. He said he was in the middle of a meeting when the phone rang, and he panicked and left the room to talk to Kevin. It's not every day that you get a call from your wife's radiation oncologist. We laugh about it now.

So the day before my supposed last radiation session, we decided that I would get three more doses. My total rads went from twenty-five to twenty-eight, a change that felt like a drop in a bucket. The day Kevin told me about the additional doses, he tried to lighten the mood. "There's a reason why they call me Dr. McMillimeter," he said. It's because he makes precise, indelible plans fighting for every millimeter of tissue or organ he can protect. After seeing this man daily for over six weeks, he tells me this nickname! Now? I could have been making fun of him the whole time.

Session twenty-eight, my last radiation cycle, finally arrived. My irradiated skin had gotten really tender at this point. Burnt to a crisp, the discoloration was a visual reminder of the "gentle healing beam". Radiation made me very tired. I wish there was a scientific explanation for it. And maybe there is, but it's beyond my ken. I hope they discover a cure for the fatigue.

I was so ready to be done. It had been a trying journey. To commemorate the completion of treatment I invited a few friends to the hospital. We shared hugs. But no tears were shed; I was all spent. Instead of it being a triumphant or bitter-sweet moment, I was resentful. Why was I given the gift of cancer? What did I do wrong? What sins was I paying for? In Hinduism we believe that the suffering we endure is karma, payment for your sins from this lifetime or a previous one. I wondered how wretched I must have been (in this lifetime or the last) that I had to pay the price with my breasts, chemo, and radiation. The end of treatment was a poignant moment, but a brief one.

I still had a job to do: thank you notes for all the radiation therapists and nurses and something special for Kevin. Nuwan and I came up with a brilliant gift: a Saints jersey. He's from New Orleans and a Saints fanatic. This was no ordinary Saints jersey, though—it was personalized and included the number 10. Kevin was thrilled when he saw it, because he loves the Saints, but he started rambling on about how "number 10 had been traded away last year . . ." I didn't interrupt because I was waiting for him to see the name on the back of the jersey. The moment he saw the name he burst out laughing. It said "MC MM" for Dr. McMillimeter. He thought the number 10 was because he was a ten, so I was sure to crush his ego before his head got too big. I reminded him that "10" was his birthday, the tenth of September. What would these physicians do without me keeping them in check?

Here's the thank you note I wrote him:

Dear Kevin,

Words fall short when I try to pen down our gratitude for you. It also doesn't help that English is my 3rd language! THANK YOU for taking a personal interest in me and ensuring I have the best shot at survival. Nuwan and I appreciate every mm you fought for to protect my organs. That didn't make the breath-hold technique on a hard metal table, in a cold room with blinding red light difficult at all. I am Super Woman after all (oh, and perfect).

Thank you for saving my life, for giving Nuwan his wife and my children their mother. I will cherish every appointment I've had with you. Your empathy, dedication, technical prowess, warm hugs, ridiculous sense of humor and HUMANITY leave me humbled and awe-inspired.

- If you find yourself in a pickle over amps or think 'Eh, she doesn't need to know about the exit beam' think this, "What would Niyati do?" and the answer will become clear. Give it a try....

- If I keep the patient waiting for over an hour because I'm behind on my dictations

- If I walk into the therapy room 10 minutes into treatment

- If I tell the patient 1 day before remission she needs 3 extra doses

Feel free to get yourself a bumper sticker, "What would NIYATI do?"

I offer you more than bumper stickers- eternal gratitude, everlasting respect, unending mockery and love. Thank you for being the Peddler of (the DNA altering) Gentle Healing Beam.

From,

Nuwan & Niyati

It might be hard to understand this, but I enjoyed my stay at Carcinoma Central (as I jokingly referred to the cancer center). Of course, I wish I'd never had the disease, but given the situation, we still had the gumption to laugh in the face of cancer. Relationships forged in the wake of trauma are long-lasting. I can understand if Kevin, Stephanie, and oncologists around the globe don't feel the same way, because they see hundreds, maybe thousands of cancer patients in their lifetime. But they will all hold a special place in my heart, and I'm eternally indebted to them. I love them, and I have made it abundantly clear that I will continue to harass them over text or email, so they never forget how much they mean to me and what an important job they do.

9. VICTIM BLAMING

"The universe doesn't allow perfection."
— Stephen Hawking, *A Brief History of Time*

Everyone deals with cancer differently. Some choose to keep the disease to themselves, and some share the news. In Indian culture there is a sense of shame associated with cancer. And I felt that shame as I started to break the news to friends. In that world, the c-word is something you hide and, if possible, pretend never happened. I've seen this in my family, with close friends and acquaintances of Indian origin who hide their cancer. I like to call it "clandestine cancer".

Breasts and cancer pose two challenges in Indian society. First there is the indignity associated with saying the word "breast" out loud. Women's reproductive parts are taboo; girls are made to feel embarrassed and are told that saying "breast" is akin to exposing them. Consequently, anything associated with breasts carries this same taboo.

I have a distinct memory of buying a bra as a teenager with my mother. The store wrapped the "contents" in a brown paper bag, the same packaging that is used for alcohol. Puberty is hard enough, but this made me feel like I was partaking in an illicit activity. Fast-forward to motherhood, when breastfeeding carries a stigma because it is considered to be immodest. Not only must it be done behind closed doors, but you are shunned from saying "*breast*feeding". It must only be referred to as feeding. Needless to say, a society that is so uncomfortable saying "breast" will have an even harder time talking about breast health.

The dichotomy here is that breasts are socially accepted as objects of sexual desire; watch any Bollywood song and dance, and it will speak volumes on this topic. But an open dialogue about breasts when talking about breast health—think mastitis, plugged ducts, discharge, or tumors—is considered inappropriate table talk.

Next is the dreaded c-word. Sitting around the dinner table, you can say, "Aunty Anula had a heart attack," but you would lower your voice and speak in code if the same beloved Aunty had been diagnosed with cancer. This is made worse when medical professionals deliver a cancer diagnosis as "CA breast," "CA lung," "CA [insert body part]." We believe that saying or thinking something unpleasant will make it come true, sort of like a self-fulfilling prophecy. I've been told that only women who talk about cancer get cancer, and that, "You must always think positive." It is easy to see that the shame associated with cancer is exacerbated when it comes to women's cancers. Breast/cervical/ovarian/uterine cancer—I call them the double whammy of taboos.

One possibly universal reason to hide the disease is to protect your children. I get this as a mother. An acquaintance told me that she had a double mastectomy followed by chemotherapy, but wanted to protect her daughter, and so she chose to hide the disease. Her daughter was eleven years old. Here's the problem: children are highly perceptive. My sweet boy, at age four, knew that I was sick. I would lay in bed and sleep a lot. Vihaan was such a darling, he would crawl into bed with me and pat my back and say, "Amma is tired. Amma is not feeling well." He knew something was wrong.

He is a sensitive young boy, and I love him so much. Just thinking about how nurturing Vihaan is brings me to tears. He grew up so quickly when he saw me unwell. The beauty of children, though, is also their resilience. As far as the word cancer was concerned, I told Vihaan this: "Vihaan, Amma has cancer. Amma needs surgery and medicine, and then I'll be all better, okay?" And he would say "Okay." Once, when Vihaan saw my mastectomy scars, he asked, "Amma, did you get an ouchie?" I told him, "Yes, but it doesn't hurt anymore. I'm all better now." I just feel like you're fooling yourself if you think you can get away with not telling your children about your sickness.

It is a mother's instinct to protect her babies from all harm. But it takes an exceptionally brave mother to tell her children the truth, help them face their fears, and prepare them for a brighter future. Even though my son was only four, I wanted him to know I had cancer. Of course, I told him, "Amma is going to be all right," which we knew was not a guarantee. But that was my version of introducing the truth to my boy. And as both kids get older I will educate them on my health and future challenges.

Another cultural aspect I have struggled with is the speculation over the cause of cancer. "It must be red meat consumption, birth control, or her modern lifestyle that caused it." This misconception will self-eradicate with greater literacy, I'm sure, but I feel more can be done to debunk the assumption that immoral or unacceptable behavior causes cancer. A scientifically accepted cause of cancer is genetics. Most of us have heard about the BRCA1 gene. But here's another problem: we Indians take genetics very personally, as though we had a choice in the matter. Saying cancer is genetic curses the family blood line. Think about arranged marriages—no one will want to marry into a family that has a history of cancer. And finally, if all other "explanations" fail, there's always the mantra of karma to fall back on, as in, "It must have been something I did."

The result of these damning notions surrounding cancer is shame. This shame is so powerful that cancer patients will chose not to get treated in Mumbai's elite Tata Memorial Hospital, because they don't want to risk running into a familiar face. Tata Memorial Hospital is synonymous with cancer care. *Everyone will know you have cancer!*

Well, I shared the news with everyone I knew, because I have watched women in my family endure cancer treatment in cloak-and-dagger fashion. Indian culture impressed upon them that cancer is a forbidden word, and that it is dishonorable to say "breast". When I started telling aunts and cousins about my diagnosis, I was forewarned: "Now don't go telling everyone. Don't post on social media. Are you sure you want everyone to know?" I was adamant that I did. Why must I carry this burden of shame associated with cancer? I did not ask for this disease. I do not deserve this.

I did refrain from social media posts, however. I begrudgingly admit that, in a small way, the Indian Hindu in me prevailed there.

As trying as the experience of admitting I had cancer was, the ultimate reward was well worth the heartache. Once my relatives and friends here saw how open I was about the disease, they jumped to my rescue. They asked about my treatment, called frequently, and put their discomfort aside. We talked about the c-word! I grabbed cancer by the balls.

• • •

Unfairly or not, women who battle cancer in secrecy propagate this cycle of shame. I could've chosen to follow this path of suffering silently, but I felt that only brings indignity to a disease that we have absolutely no control over. I take pride in my forthrightness, but I paid the price as victim blamers and callous commentators started to surface in my life. Instead of writing some poignant book about my cancer journey, I was seriously considering writing one called *The Shit*

People Say When They Hear You Have Cancer. I know, the title needs a bit of work—but you get the point.

Fair warning here: the rest of this chapter contains cursing. Liberal amounts of it. There are some situations in life where profanity is needed, and describing your suffering and the ignorance of other people is one of them.

There's a tie between the top two comments I received—tied for first place in heartlessness, that is. First, "What's the prognosis?" Asking a patient their prognosis is another way of asking them what their chances of survival are. That's a touch heartless, I'd say. Would you ask an eighty-year-old how many good years she has left? Do you see a premature baby and ask the parents if the baby will make it through the night? It's a marvel (or so I think) that I was asked this question by friends, random strangers, and fellow survivors. The lack of humanity was astounding. When the umpteenth colleague asked me what my prognosis was, I said to her, "If you're asking whether I'm going to live or die, I'm going to fucking live."

"I've heard you don't lose hair during chemotherapy" is the other first-place winner. It seemed like everyone knew somebody who didn't lose their hair during chemotherapy. The reports were ridiculous. And those claims, truthful or not, gave false hope—to my mother and sister. When I asked Stephanie if I was going to lose my hair, she told me point blank, "YES." She said I would lose my hair, my eyebrows, and my eyelashes. She didn't mince words. She wanted me to be prepared, because she has seen the reality.

Here's the problem with people that peddle the no-hair-loss-in-chemotherapy line: they inadvertently instill shame in hair loss. What is the first sign that someone has cancer? The hairless, scarf-wearing, no-brow-and-lashes-having, pale look of a chemotherapy patient. And that is the worst fear of friends and family, to see you like that. It exposes their vulnerability, which tells me they are uncomfortable seeing me like that. It is deceptively reassuring for loved ones to hear, "Not all people lose their hair during chemotherapy." While that might be true, it inspires prayers to the Almighty for the one thing that *will* eventually be restored. The true tragedy of my cancer was the double mastectomy. My medical care team was going to surgically remove my breasts in order to give me the best chance at survival. Does the temporary loss of hair still sound important? The difference is that chemo-induced baldness is a visible reminder of cancer. It makes other people uneasy and anxious. The double mastectomy, on the other hand, is under my shirt and out of sight.

The array of insensitive comments wasn't limited to the completely ignorant. People who should know better were often just as guilty. When a sweet childhood friend, now a doctor in Vancouver, learned about my diagnosis, she was shocked. Her first question to me, after learning that I had completed seven cycles of chemotherapy and had a double mastectomy and lymph node dissection, was, "Are you having any side effects from the treatment?" I'll admit that I don't have much of a filter, but this really pushed me over the edge. I responded, and I quote, "I thought you were a physician in Canada. What do you think happens with chemotherapy? Radiation is no walk in the park either. And a double mastectomy has the minor side effect of no boobs."

When you tell people you have cancer, everyone has a story of someone they knew who had it too. Some of the stories I heard, however, were far from encouraging. A friend told me that his uncle had pancreatic cancer, and that the doctors only gave him six months to live. I naïvely thought this meant he was doing well; he then went on to tell me that his uncle lived a year longer than his doctors predicted. Well, thanks for letting me know! This became a pattern. Another friend told me that her mother-in-law had Stage 4 cancer and lived three years longer than they thought. I was so confused; why would people tell me such tragic stories? Either these friends had already made up their minds that I was dying, and so they were attempting to give me examples of people who had unexpectedly been given more time on earth; or they were genuinely so senseless that they didn't realize telling a cancer patient stories of people dying with cancer is not an encouraging thing to do. A few times, awkwardly enough, I was told, "Get well soon." How should I respond to that? "Get well soon" is something I would say to a person who has a cold. "Get well soon" is not what you tell cancer patients; at minimum, it's in comically bad taste and sure made Nuwan and me laugh. *You have cancer, get well soon, ha-ha-ha?*

A highly educated friend with a double master's degree in science texted me confidently that, "Breast cancer is 100% curable," and urged me not to worry. I was dismayed when I read that. Hell, a tweaked back and some spinal misalignment isn't 100 percent curable. But this friend, in her infinite wisdom, declared breast cancer 100 percent curable. I know all she wanted to do was encourage me, but it is still a strange thing to say, since it couldn't be farther from the truth. Cancer is an inexplicable disease, one that has several risk factors but no known direct cause. It's a disease that has no cure, even if scientists believe we will get closer to achieving permanent remission with drugs and treatment (and, eventually, a cure).

Another friend heard about my diagnosis and messaged me this: "Hoping for the best because I think you've got a decent shot at it." *I was told I have "a decent shot".* I told her that she severely underestimated me, and that I was going to beat this. I stood up for myself almost every time. And it was exhausting.

A girlfriend asked me if I was afraid that I passed it on to my daughter while breastfeeding. Let me get this straight: since it's *breast* cancer, and I was breastfeeding, that must be how cancer spreads? Stupidity knows no bounds. I told her, "No, I am afraid it's genetic, and I intend on keeping up with new medical advice. I will get my daughter *and son* tested as we learn more about the disease."

One day I was at the salon post-cancer treatment for some pampering. The stylist is someone I've known for years. This is the conversation I had with her.

> Stylist: "Does your surgery mean you can't breastfeed?"

> Me: "The mastectomy? Yes, yes. That means I cannot breastfeed. No breast tissue, no breast."

> Stylist: "So, you don't have nipples either?" [Possibly thinking that if I had nipples, even without breast tissue, there would be milk?]

> Me: "Some women get to keep their nipples, depending on the cancer staging and size of the tumor. But no, I don't have nipples."

> Stylist: "The reconstruction then, it's just for show?"

This is one of those epic conversations that needed to be recorded in a book. Sometimes I wonder if I'm writing this book just to document *The Shit People Say When They Hear You Have Cancer*. Maybe I am.

A few morons asked Nuwan if I was feeling better with chemotherapy. I put that in the ignoramus bucket. Chemotherapy isn't some vitamin-infused water or protein shake that, over time, will make you stronger. Chemotherapy is the decimator, poison in the veins, a cocktail of drugs that kills everything in its path. But maybe these savants thought that chemotherapy is energy-giving? Or they are simpletons, who think that since cancer made me sick, chemotherapy would make me feel better.

I know I'm venting in this chapter, but bear with me. You can do this. Continue reading and, of course, don't forget to laugh. If you find yourself wondering, "Is Niyati making this shit up?" The answer is, "No. I am not. This all really happened."

Still, the worst experiences I had were with the victim blamers. I was asked questions like, "How come you detected it so late?"; "How long did you wait to report the lump?"; "Didn't you feel any symptoms?"; "Did you feel tired or lose weight?"; or "Was it because you were breastfeeding that the lump went undetected?"

Despite their breathtaking callousness, I defended myself. I repeatedly explained that breastfeeding was probably *the* reason I felt the lump at all. Women are most aware of their breasts during breastfeeding, and hormonal changes can help make the symptoms present sooner. I didn't "wait" to report the lump; between my lump detection, mammogram, biopsy, and cancer diagnosis, only five days went by. And I never felt fatigued. Just before my diagnosis we had taken the children to Disney World, where we clocked 28,000–32,000 steps a day while pushing two strollers.

People asked me what lifestyle changes I was going to make now that I had cancer, such as eating organic or limiting red meat. Check and check: I don't eat red meat, and most of the groceries in my house are organic. I pay through my nose to buy organic chicken and organic milk. (Speaking of milk, a concerned friend told me she watched a Netflix documentary which said that consuming too much dairy can cause cancer, and she asked if I was going to change my diet.) Other than during my pregnancy, I've never weighed more than a hundred pounds. I try to lead a healthy life, I don't heat my food in plastic Tupperware, and when I read about carcinogens, I try to eliminate them. Yet I got breast cancer, so go figure.

• • •

We live in a world where victim blaming is almost customary. Rape victims are asked what underwear they were wearing at the time of their assault. College girls are questioned about the number of beers they drank. All of this takes the blame off the perpetrator and places it on the victim. Suggestive clothing, a thong, too many beverages—take your pick.

I talked to both Kevin and Stephanie about the toll victim blamers took on me. Stephanie speculated women often ask "how" and "why" questions, because they don't want cancer to happen to them. They think, *If I do my annual checks and mammograms, I will not get the disease.* Or, *Niyati must've ignored the obvious symptoms, and that's why the disease progressed.* They are afraid that my situation could become their reality, so they want to make sense of it. *If I follow all the rules, then I won't get cancer.* The victim blaming is a form of self-preservation, a way to make sense of a senseless disease. What I know now is that cancer is cruel, it is equal-opportunity, and it is relentless. And that's what makes it scary.

As bad as lots of the comments were, at least most people meant well, I believe. But others said things with a vaguely condescending tone, like, "At least you get to live," or, "It's just boobs." These comments minimized my suffering and were deeply hurtful. Kevin advised that, if the situation allowed, I should tell people how I felt when they were being unsympathetic. He said that I went through an amputation, and that they weren't "just breasts"—they were parts of my body that I no longer have. And that I was allowed to mourn the loss, a profound loss.

Catharine was another helpful sounding board. Whenever I was upset and I texted her, she would affirm my feelings and tell me that I was allowed to be upset, and that what happened to us this year as a family sucked.

I experienced a unique case of victim blaming while I was helping a friend get a biopsy following her first mammogram. I went to the Breast Health Center in Columbus, the exact place of my diagnosis, to give Ana company. On my drive to the center for her visit my heart was racing. I had flashbacks of the parking lot, Nuwan and I being there, how battered I felt after the biopsy, and how naïve I was to think that was the worst of it. But I wanted to be there for my friend. My life's goal is to give back. I had to do this.

The Center let me go in with her, and after she changed, we sat and talked. Ana asked about chemotherapy, but I tried to rein her thoughts in to the present. One step at a time, let's cross the bridge when we come to it—pick your metaphor. I told her again that everything was going to be okay.

"How come you detected your cancer so late?" she asked.

There it was: victim blaming at its cruelest. I defended myself, told her my timeline again (even though she knew it), and explained that I had reported it right away.

"Did the tumor feel sore? Were you tired all the time?"

I answered all of Ana's questions, tried to put her mind at ease. I told her she was not alone, that I was right there for her. But again, I was put in a position where I felt the need to defend myself.

Ana's tests came out negative. I was, and am, thankful for that, and we celebrated her all-clear! She is now an ally in the community, helping other cancer patients who are going through treatment.

● ● ●

The reality, as I touched on earlier, is that, despite all our advances in cancer treatment, the disease still doesn't have a cure. In fact, oncologists don't even use the word "cured" when they deem you cancer-free. Instead, you're said to be "in remission." You are in remission till the disease recurs, or in permanent remission if it never comes back. It amazed me when friends and even strangers had tears in their eyes when I told them I had cancer. I would wonder to myself if maybe this person had lost someone dear to them, or if they were survivors themselves. The tears flowed from everyone, from grown men to older women, from cousins, aunts, and uncles. These people did not victim blame. Their compassion and love for me were condition-free and gave me strength. The victim-blaming, ignorant, and insensitive people were but a minority. And in the grand scheme of things they faded into the background.

An engineer who used to work for me, Alex, sent me this message: "You are very loved, my friend. When Kruthi told me, I had tears coming out. Somehow I have made you out to be super-human in my head, like someone I can always fall back on. You are loved and admired." Alex and his wife Bridgette babysat Aarini for us on several weekends during my treatment. They have a young baby girl at home. On the Sundays that Aarini spent with the Cruz family, she was spoiled rotten. I once asked Alex if Aarini played with their dog, Tyrion; he replied, "Your daughter has never touched the ground." Alex would hold Aarini the whole time. She would play and sleep on Alex. She felt safe in his arms. For her part, Bridgette devised the most organized meal delivery plan one can imagine. Once a week she would drop off an insulated bag full of containers of meals. She always included a note, disposable silverware, and heating instructions. How do you repay this kindness? If imitation is the highest form of flattery, then it's Bridgette's generosity of spirit that I will spend a lifetime trying to mimic. Priya and my sister-in-law Priyanka both commented on how this would never happen anywhere else in the world, not in India, not in the UK. Nuwan and I are lucky to be in Columbus, in a community of engineers and physicians, immigrants and Americans, who are fiercely loyal, generous, and empathetic.

Even now, some nights, I lay in bed feeling unworthy of this outpouring of love and support. I think about all the people involved in my treatment: the oncologist, radiation oncologist, breast surgeon, plastic surgeon, OB/ GYN, radiation therapists, ultrasound technician, immunotherapist, radiologist, nurses, nurse navigators, and anesthesiologist. It has taken so many care providers to give me a fighting chance at life. All this expertise to ensure that cancer doesn't claim a life. How can a single life be this valuable that so many people worked together to save it? It's *just one* life. Vikram said that if I were in India, I would've been dead by now. I think he was implying that the staging and grading of my cancer would leave Indian doctors with little hope and motivation to fight for me. Maybe he is correct; maybe not. But I do know that the way cancer is treated in the US is unparalleled. The standard of care and emphasis on minimizing suffering is unparalleled. I am fortunate to be in this country. God bless the United States of America.

10. IT TAKES A VILLAGE

**"I feel the embrace of freedom in a thousand
bonds of delight."**
— Rabindranath Tagore, *Gitanjali*

There's a saying that has resurfaced in recent years: "It takes a village to raise a child." It means that children thrive when the community comes together and helps the new parents. This applies just as much to battling cancer. The treatment is physically demanding, emotionally draining, and time-critical. The medical jargon, treatment options, chemotherapy schedule, and myriad of prescription drugs can get overwhelming. Doing this alone would be like going into a battlefield unarmed and without backup. If it takes a village to raise a child, it takes a bloody army to battle cancer.

I had an army of people behind me, all of them supporting Nuwan and me through this life-altering phase. It all started with the medical team. The nurse at my OB/GYN's office, Tracy, insisted on an ultrasound and mammogram for my lumps, though she could've easily shrugged them off as benign cysts and sent me home. But she didn't. Then came the radiologist, Dr. Matthews, who told me directly that it was not a cyst. Had Dr. Matthews let me go home without the biopsy, or Tracy not insisted on an ultrasound, the cancer would have continued to wreak havoc inside my body, endangering me further. I have spoken to many survivors and read online forums related to cancer detection, and it's alarming how many premenopausal women fall through the cracks. So I am thankful to nurse Tracy and to Dr. Matthews for helping to detect my cancer.

When my colleagues and friends found out about my breast cancer diagnosis, they quickly moved past the initial shock and volunteered to help. It was like mobilizing an army. This is the part where the victim blamers fade into the background. Help arrived on many different fronts: childcare, meals, groceries, and accompanying me to the hospital if Nuwan needed to be with the children. I once had a 7:00 a.m. appointment with the cardiologist for an EKG before my port-a-cath surgery. We couldn't get a sitter that early in the day, so Nuwan was going to drop the kids off at daycare early, and then join me at the hospital. I didn't want to go to that appointment alone. I asked for company, and my friend Aiswarya volunteered. On the way to the hospital I said to her, "Whenever Nuwan and I drive by the hospital, we talk about how we had both our children here. And now, this place is tainted. This hospital is now a reminder of my cancer."

"Every time you have been to the hospital you came back stronger," said Aiswarya. "You will come out stronger this time too." Her confidence in my recovery bolstered my courage.

There's nothing to be gained by suffering in silence. If I had driven myself that morning, I would not have had this conversation with Aiswarya. Columbus Hospital means the world to us, and whenever we have visitors over, Nuwan and I make sure we drive past the hospital and show where Vihaan and Aarini were born. Aiswarya's comment helped to put a positive light on the situation and led me to reconnect my experience there with happier associations.

I'm a planner, and I like to be organized. So when my life started spiraling out of control I felt the urge to make a plan and straighten things out. Doing this gave me some small semblance of control, which counted for something. So I turned to Microsoft Excel—thank you, Mr. Gates—and *Excel*ed my way through cancer, pun intended. I brainstormed all the friends I could call on for help and then categorized them. The categories were: Childcare, Errands, Meal Delivery, Work, and Miscellaneous. Broadly speaking my friends got divided into three buckets:

1. **Friends with kids our age.** I scheduled playdates with them and asked a few to serve as emergency contacts if things came up unexpectedly, which happened more than once.

2. **Single friends and friends without children.** I requested this group help with meals, errands, grocery delivery, following up on insurance, and more.

3. **Colleagues.** I reached out to colleagues if I needed someone to cover a meeting or get something rescheduled. I asked them to help me with HR paperwork and disability services.

Besides all this I needed to delegate a meal coordinator, someone who would take over organizing all the people who had offered their help. Aiswarya, Bhargav and Kruthi took on this mammoth task. Several people had offered to send us homecooked meals regularly, so Kruthi coordinated deliveries for four times a week, with a rotation system between ten-odd friends and acquaintances. Strangers became friends, and friends became family. Kruthi gave strict instructions: use disposable Tupperware, so that Niyati and Nuwan don't need to sort out returns; leave the food at their doorstep (don't expect a welcome party while they are going through something so difficult); and other rules that I can only speculate on. It was so touching to hear from Kruthi that she had gotten an overwhelming response from people who wanted to deliver more meals and to help in other ways. As a result Nuwan and I were treated to homecooked food for four months, with enough leftovers to ration and eat for a few more months.

I was and will always be humbled by the outpouring of support. Not a day goes by without me feeling that I don't deserve so much kindness, that it's too much for one individual. The whole community came together for us. The generosity of people in the Midwest, immigrants and citizens alike, is incomparable.

Pallav was the designated errand boy. That poor chap isn't just a hardworking engineer; he was also doing a part-time master's in engineering. I handed him the task of groceries. While there's an online grocery shopping option in our area, I've always found the produce it provides to be subpar. It's better when someone picks that out. So Pallav delivered groceries almost on a weekly basis. I had transferred a decent chunk of change to his bank account to cover the costs, and Pallav said that he would give me the receipts from his trips so we could keep a tally. Offended, I said, "Absolutely not, Pallav. You keep the tally and give me back the remainder once we are done with treatment." Checking receipts would cheapen our friendship. Pallav also sorted out insurance claims for me that were convoluted or stuck in the system. That was a huge help.

A staggering number of people stepped up to help us. I attribute this to two things. One, I was transparent and completely honest about my diagnosis from the beginning. People can't offer help if they don't know you are in a crisis situation. Two, I asked for help—verbatim, out loud, in writing, over texts and phone calls, I asked people to help me. That requires vulnerability.

Before my cancer, I equated vulnerability with weakness. Being vulnerable and raw to the world made me feel exposed and put me completely out of my comfort zone. No one likes asking for help. But during my ordeal I decided I would just have to work through my discomfort. Vulnerability meant talking about my fears, facing my own mortality, dealing with body-image issues, letting people in but being firm about boundaries. And yes, there was some show of emotion, an occasional tear or two. Vulnerability meant walking around with no cloak. But it also meant allowing others in, others without whom I couldn't beat cancer.

This chapter of my life was an open book, and that didn't stop after my treatment was over. Hence the reason behind writing this book. I hope the vulnerability and courage I have shown in the face of adversity is a source of inspiration for others. It took this cancer for me to understand that it takes tremendous courage to be vulnerable. Vulnerability is not a sign of weakness, as I used to think. In actuality, only the brave dare to be vulnerable.

• • •

I f cancer is war, my commander-in-chief was Nuwan. As I've said, he is always by my side. Nuwan wasn't just physically present for my doctor's appointments and consultations; he was mentally there too. He listened, analyzed, and asked questions. He inquired about side effects, pain management, treatment options, and the path to permanent remission. Moreover, he often had to act as a single parent to our children. The rest of what he endured, I can only imagine.

My mother came to the US twice from India during my treatment, once during chemotherapy and the second time during radiation. Her visit during chemotherapy was crucial, and of enormous help. Aarini had been weaned abruptly, and I could no longer co-sleep with her. Aai took over the reins, spending innumerable sleepless nights bottle-feeding and soothing Aarini. She helped wean her. Aai also did endless baskets of laundry and cooked for us. She did this while watching her daughter battle chemotherapy. She did this as she witnessed all my hair fall off. It took a tremendous toll on my mother. No mother should ever have to watch their child suffer. Life is inherently cruel. But my mother was there for us through thick and thin.

The greatest sacrifice and act of kindness came from my big sister Priyadarshini. Priya had given birth to her second child, a daughter, on November 2, 2017. When she found out about my cancer she vowed to be here to help me through it, at any cost. She paid a hefty price to keep that promise. She left her breastfeeding infant behind with her husband, Kamlesh. Their son was four years old then, so my brother-in-law was left at home with both children. My sister extended her maternity leave to unpaid leave and put her life on hold to come here and be a mother to my children while I underwent surgery. I cannot imagine how incredibly hard it must have been for her to leave her children behind. I am in awe of her supportive husband and in-laws for encouraging her and telling her to not worry about the kids, that they would take care of everything back home. Priya breastfed Rajvika till a week before the visit. I felt terrible about the ordeal I put her through.

As I predicted, Priya was shocked when she first saw me post-chemo. Even though we had been Face Timing often, Priya had no idea what a terrible toll chemotherapy had taken on my body. It didn't just break her heart; it crushed her soul. But this made her even more determined to help me. She hit the ground running, taking the kids off my hands and letting me rest. She took over the kitchen and started cooking healthy, sumptuous meals for us. She came to all my doctor's appointments.

Priya and I would catch up during the day and talk about life, what to make of the cancer, how this happened to *us*, and how she wasn't going to let anything happen to me. She took care of everything. She came two weeks before surgery, wanting to use that time to learn each kid's routine and have them become familiar with her. She pumped breastmilk day and night, and we stored it in the freezer. She has an unwavering faith in God. She had no doubt whatsoever that chemotherapy would work, and

I would have a pathologic complete response (PCR).

Kamlesh gave Priya the courage she needed to leave their newborn behind. He told Priya that her top priority should be *my* children and supporting us through the cancer treatment. He told her that he would take care of everything on the home front. Their son was acutely aware of the fact that Aai was going to be away for a while. Kamlesh had his hands full; he was a single parent to two kids while my sister came to help us. He was a pillar of strength during this ordeal and did not allow Priya to be nervous about being away from the kids. I am blessed to have Kamlesh for a brother-in-law.

In time I lifted the ban on males that I had been enforcing in the house, because I had started to accept my new, bruised body. My aunt Bharati *maushi* (maushi means maternal aunt in Marathi) and uncle Prabhat *kaka* (kaka is uncle in Marathi) came from Stamford, Connecticut for an entire week after my surgery to help with chores and to take me to my daily radiation treatments. Prabhat *kaka* cooked the most decadent, yet healthy meals and gourmet salads. Bharati *maushi* helped me spray green tea solution on my irradiated chest, and applied steroid cream on the skin that had started to burn. Soon after their visit my uncle Ravi *kaka* and aunt Ujwala *kaku* (*kaku* is aunt in Marathi) visited from Maryland. It was Ujwala *kaku's* second visit, and she was happy to see an uptick in my energy levels. It was a welcome relief to have my aunts and uncles over.

People from all corners of my life made great sacrifices for me. How can I ever repay this kindness and generosity? Clearly I can't, but I intend to pay it forward for the rest of my life—to pay it forward, give back, help wherever I can, and be a better version of me.

11. FIRE IN MY SOUL

**"A girl's love for her father. Immutable.
Unbearable but unbreakable."**
— Kristin Hannah, *The Nightingale*

I had come home from jujitsu class a proud green belt. "Baba, I graduated today," I said to my father. "I can break a brick with my bare hands!" I was twelve years old. My father replied in Hindi, "Sure you did, darling." *Sarcasm? Was that sarcasm?* Offended, I said, "You don't believe me? Bring me a brick, and I'll show you." Priya and Aai watched this exchange unfold, aghast.

We lived on the third floor of a seven-story building in the Bombay Port Trust (BPT) Colony apartment complex. My father called a friend and asked for a brick. I can only imagine how that conversation went: "Hi, do you have a brick? Oh, nothing. I just want to see if my youngest can break it with her bare fist." This was totally normal for a nonviolent, vegetarian Hindu household.

We got the brick. I was livid. My father doubted my strength. I'd show him. Picture this: a scrawny brown girl with neatly braided hair down to her waist, fuming at the ears. When I say "scrawny" I mean it: skin and bone. Remember, I've been hailed as having the upper-body strength of linguine—as an adult. Baba's doubts were justified. The brick was brought to me. I got into position and yelled "Hiyaaaaa!" as I attacked it with all my rage. The brick did not break. I couldn't believe it didn't crumble under my fist of fury. My hand wasn't bruised, but my ego was. I said to Baba sheepishly, "I want to try again." He told me he had no doubt that I could break this brick, and that I ought to try again. The brick was positioned on two cinder blocks. With my father's vote of confidence I went, "Hiyaaaaa!" once again. And I broke that brick in half.

This is one of my proudest childhood memories. The sense of accomplishment and pride I feel comes from the fact that I failed at first, but dared to try again. And that made my father proud. The beauty of childhood and its innocence is being unafraid of failure. I don't know when that changes, but I believe it has to do with age. Shame becomes so powerful that, instead of trying something new and putting ourselves out there, the fear of rejection or failure makes us hesitate. And this shame manifests itself in bigger things.

• • •

The following year we planned a big family holiday. I was then thirteen years old, and my sister was sixteen. First we would visit my maternal grandmother, aunts, uncles, and cousins in Nagpur. And then we would celebrate Diwali in Raigarh, with my paternal grandparents, aunts and uncles. My mother was unable to join us because of work obligations (a physician's life is demanding).

It was a crisp autumn morning—November 7, 1996, to be exact—when Baba, Priya, and I got into a tuk-tuk (rickshaw) to head to the train station. We had spent a few days in Nagpur, and then it was time for us to head to Raigarh. That day was the first day of Diwali, *Dhanteras*, the Hindu festival of lights, which also happened to be my father's birthday. Diwali marks the victory of good over evil, triumphant light that eliminates darkness. And it's five days long. The only way a billion Hindus around the world can do justice to this important festival is by celebrating it over five days. Each day has a distinct significance, with specific rituals and traditions that are followed. The third day of the festival, *Lakshmi Pooja*, is widely recognized as the most important. We pray to Lakshmi, the Hindu goddess of prosperity. In preparation for the holiday Hindus decorate their homes with lamps and lights. We also shoot fireworks, wear vibrant traditional clothes, and exchange gifts of dry fruits, Indian desserts, and gold. Children also get three weeks off school! Priya and I loved Diwali and always celebrated it in a big way.

When the rickshaw pulled up in front of my grandmother's house I promptly took the window seat. My father asked me to move to the middle, so that he could sit by the window. Also, it's safer to be in the middle of a rickshaw, because the sides don't have doors or windows; it's just open. Obedient Indian kids never talk back to their parents, so as soon as I was asked to move to the middle, I did.

After that my memory is blurred. Later I was told that a drunk truck driver collided with our rickety rickshaw without windows, doors, or seatbelts, and that we were thrown from it. A couple of college students making their way to school witnessed the crash and came running to help us. I told them to contact my grandmother Kamal Koli, gave them her phone number and address, and then passed out from a concussion.

I don't recall when I came back to consciousness, but I remember a dark hospital room. Hospitals have this sterile smell that you never forget. The bed was uncomfortable, the pillow had no give, and my head hurt. The room was dimly lit. I remember my mother speaking to someone saying, "Ravi *kaka* is on his way to India." In my fleeting state of consciousness, I remember thinking, *Wow, this will be fun! My closest uncle Ravi kaka will join us for Diwali from the US. I miss him so much.* Then I passed out again.

The next time my eyes were open, my mother was by my bedside, still. She said—and I remember this distinctly— "I have some bad news for you. Your father is not doing well. He died in the car crash."

I remember feeling nothing. The news didn't register. I didn't cry. I went back to sleep. I had sustained several injuries in the crash, including a fractured right collar bone and a broken left wrist. I also had a massive concussion from the impact. My next memory is of going into surgery. An orthopedic surgeon needed to insert a pin in my left wrist to help it heal. Once I was out of surgery, I saw my mother talking to a nurse about what to do with the all the blood in my hair. The nurse recommended that we wash it out as soon as possible. She said that if the blood dried up, they would have to shave my head. Aai didn't want me to lose my luscious locks, so she washed the blood out of my hair in the bathroom sink. I cannot imagine how it feels to be a mother as red water streams out of your daughter's hair. But she was strong and did what was needed.

I noticed that my sister was in the same room as me. Her injuries were more minor, but she had a huge laceration on the side of her face, and she needed surgery to get that stitched up. We should've asked for a plastic surgeon, but this was Nagpur, and our options were limited. An incompetent surgeon stitched up the side of Priya's beautiful face as if it were a sack of rice. I remember being mad that we were in Nagpur, a small town with a small pool of surgeons.

The concussion continued to make me sleepy. My body had gone through physical trauma, and I faded in and out of awareness. Someone said to my mother, "If she doesn't see his body, this will not be real to her. She will not get closure. You must wake her up." My mother woke me up and said, "We must go to your father's funeral."

I found myself in a room full of family members. Two uncles from the US were there, along with a village's worth of people from Raigarh and

Nagpur, my grandparents, my mother, and my sister. Everyone was crying. In my culture we mourn our hearts out; tears are shed indiscriminately. You are not only given the opportunity to emote, it is expected. In the middle of the room lay my father, motionless, wrapped in a white cloth. I noticed cotton balls in his nostrils and his closed eyes. It was real. I had lost my father. I cried because everyone was crying. I was still in a state of shock, and this seemed too cruel to be true. Plus, with my concussions, who knew if this was real? Maybe it was a bad dream.

In Hinduism the body is cremated. Everyone, including my sister, went to the cremation. But I was asked to return to my hospital bed, since the journey to the funeral home was too treacherous given my fragile condition. So I went back to my hospital room and slept. A lot. When I woke my mind would only wander in one direction. I had lost my father at the age of thirteen, on his birthday, because he chose the side seat in a rickshaw and put me in the middle. He sustained the worst of the injuries. If I had protested, and said that I wanted to be by the window, it would have been me wrapped in that white cloth. But as I said, there is no tolerance for backtalk in my culture. Your parent asks you to do something, you abide. Nevertheless, I will regret that day for the rest of my life. Why didn't I speak up and say that I wanted the window seat? Yes, I'm aware this is textbook survivor's guilt. But the feeling is as true and palpable now as it's ever been.

• • •

This event, the loss of a parent, gave Priya and me a new identity: girls without a father. I cannot decide what is considered more shameful, being diagnosed with cancer or being a fatherless daughter. Common sense and logic would beg, "*Neither!*" How could losing a parent to a tragic car crash possibly bring shame? Well, in India, having a father is of utmost importance in society. It means two things. One, the family's daughters will marry well. And two, your mother isn't a widow.

Having a father means that there will be a sizeable dowry for marriage. A father is the head of the household and the primary breadwinner. If he's no more, how will the widowed mother come up with a lump sum of money to ensure that the daughters get married?

Anyone who challenges the notion of a dowry upon reading this, or points out that dowries are illegal in India, is simply deluded. Yes, dowries are officially illegal in India, but the practice of giving and receiving them is still widely practiced. For a wedding gift, instead of sending cash, the girl's parents now buy the new couple an apartment or new car. They send the girl with cases of gold jewelry, all of which become the property of the in-laws—as is the daughter-in-law. If she is allowed to work, her income goes to her in-laws. Parents with daughters are acutely aware of what they need to save for their marriage(s). Most of the time it is more than what you would save for college.

Women in India are treated as second-class citizens. Widows are a class below that. They are stigmatized and considered to be a bad omen. The social hierarchy goes like this: man, male child, female child, mother, several layers of other relations, then widow. My mother, an educated, successful, talented, beautiful woman became a widow. And on top of that great tragedy, she had no sons.

After my father died, not having a man of the house started to affect our social standing. It started small, but it still hurt. Every now and then there was a wedding that the entire BPT Colony was invited to, but we were singled out and not invited. You can't have a widow witnessing the start of a marriage, you see; it will curse the couple's happiness. The Patel family, who lived in our building, had a daughter named Preeti, who was getting married. In the run-up to the wedding, my girlfriends talked about what they were all going to wear, oblivious to the fact that I wasn't invited. I pretended that I was going to see them there and talked about what traditional clothes I was going to wear. My plan was to tell my friends that I was sick right before the event and thus couldn't come. I didn't have the heart to tell them that we were not invited, and that it was probably because my mother was a widow. I got good at lying and making up stories.

A year after the wedding, like clockwork, Preeti had a baby girl. One night, at 2 a.m., our phone rang. It was the Patel family, frantic. They told my mother there was something wrong with the baby, and that they needed help. Without hesitating for a second my mother took her stethoscope and medicine bag and rushed to their home. She was back an hour later. The baby was going to be okay, she said. For me that meant my mother had saved the baby's life.

The following morning, I had a fight with Aai. "The Patels thought you were a bad omen for the wedding," I said, "but when it came to saving their granddaughter's life, your widow-ness is forgotten? That's convenient. Why did you rush out in the middle of the night? There are eight other physicians in BPT. They could've called any of them. You know, the ones who also got invited to the wedding." I vented. I rambled. I was mad. But I stand by my statement. I thought I had made a fair point.

"This is my duty. I am a doctor, and it is my duty to help people in duress," said Aai.

I didn't care one bit for her all-forgiving demeanor and moral lesson on right and wrong. I didn't care one bit for the Patels and all those who ostracized us because we had lost our father. I was bitter. And I admit I still am. I ought to start reading books on forgiveness, Gandhi, and meditation, right?

Another incident of discrimination sticks out in my memory. During

Hindu festivals, women in BPT Colony gathered for prayers and celebration. One such joyous occasion was Holi, the Hindu festival of color that marks the first day of spring. During the festival adults and children alike smear colored powder on each other, throw water balloons, and spray each other with water. It was Holi, and my sister and I went outside with our colored powder and water balloons. My mother was just about ready to step out of the house when the doorbell rang. During the festival, it's customary for women to knock on doors and ask people to come outside and join them, Aai expected to be greeted by a crowd. When she opened the door, though, all she saw was one woman. All the ladies had run away except that one, who wasn't fast enough. "Oh, I'm sorry," that neighbor said to my mother, and quickly headed to the stairs.

My mother hid this incident from Priya and me for several years. She wanted to ensure that our Holi wasn't ruined as our Diwali had been. I'm not sure why the neighbor said "sorry". She could've just put some color on my mother and asked her to join them. Instead she chose to shun her.

Vacations also got tricky for the three of us. When traveling within India we always got asked, "The three of you . . . are you traveling alone?" How is three people considered "alone"? It was because we were three women. Where was the man of the house? It became second nature for my sister and me to say, "Our father is away on a work trip, so it is just us." It was easier to lie and be treated as a full family unit than to say we had lost our father and get treated as a lesser family.

These experiences defined my sister and me. It defined my mother. What kind of a society alienates a woman and her two teenage daughters when they have been struck by such tragedy? My mother told us that it was important to be strong, never to show weakness or to wallow in self-pity. The world can be a wretched place, but she taught us to be unafraid. I carry these lessons to this day, and they have helped me to stay strong in the face of adversity. Aai wanted us both to get educated, earn a living (or, as she said, "Stand on your own two feet."), travel, experience the world, and succeed. She reminded us that we were where we were because she had a job. And that if we were in her village, or, really, any small town in India, we would've been married off by the age of twenty to an older man for the inadequate dowry we had.

I don't recall much of what my sister went through. Priya was a silent sufferer. She was busy making sure I had everything I needed to succeed. Are you wondering what it means to be a sixteen-year-old worried about your thirteen-year-old baby sister? It meant the following: Priya would sharpen my pencils and fill ink into my pens the night before exams. She would make sure my geometry box had a compass, protractor, and whatever else was needed. Priya checked to see if I had the logarithmic table in my book bag. If it was Sports Day, she would make sure my sports uniform was laundered and my canvas shoes were painted. I was a spoiled baby sister.

I had missed a month of school due to my injuries, but the Catholic school I went to had strict rules. So what if you lost a parent? There's no excuse for missing class, homework submissions, and midterms. This actually served me well; schoolwork kept my mind occupied and made me determined to not fall behind. I had a fire in me, one that would either illuminate or consume. I had something to prove, and I used academics as a coping mechanism. I later used this life hack during my cancer journey. Working during chemo kept me mentally strong. I've come full circle.

I am still in touch with my elementary school friends who watched me come back after losing a parent. I reached out to one such friend, Suma (the one who now lives in Seattle), after my diagnosis. The news brought her to tears while she was at work. Here's a handwritten note she sent me in support.

Niyati my dear friend,

I am sorry that you and the kids and Nuwan have to go
through what you're going through & I wish I could do
something other than write you this note.

I wanted to remind you of the <u>immense</u> strength & resilience
you (and your family) have shown in the past, in the face of
great tragedy. You had to develop grit & strength & courage at
a very young age—and it's still there inside you & it's going to
help you fight this like no one else can.

I remember thinking to myself (in school and now), I'm so
proud & inspired by this girl my age who's dealing with life
with the grace & maturity of an enlightened soul.

Look within you for the strength you need—it's there

Look around you for the support you need—we're here

Look at your beautiful kids & husband for the motivation…

And when this is all over, a bad nightmare, we'll remember to
be grateful for another day.

I'm rooting for you.

Love,

Suma

Sometimes I feel like I've been able to take on cancer because I am a
fearless, fatherless daughter. I think Suma would agree.

12. CHANGING MY NARRATIVE

> **"Respect was invented to cover the empty place
> where love should be."**
> — Leo Tolstoy, *Anna Karenina*

W e were at Mumbai International Airport. My mother seldom gets emotional, but she had tears in her eyes. I told her not to cry, and that I would be back, that I'd finish my education at Ohio State University and return. As I walked away, though, I knew I would never live in India again. We were treated unfairly in *my* country, by *my* people, at a time when we needed the most support. I would never return to that society. And I would never marry into an Indian family that gave so much importance to a woman's marital status. I know those seem like very bold statements coming from an eighteen-year-old who hadn't seen the world; but I was about to step into the world, alone—with the financial and emotional support of my family, but alone. And I knew certain truths about my life. I may have been young, but I knew who I was.

When I began my undergraduate studies at Ohio State, it had approximately 55,000 students enrolled (undergraduate and graduate), making it one of the largest colleges in the US. The university boasted about its diversity and international student programs, so when I arrived,

I was expecting to see people of all ethnicities, races, and religions. My reality, though, couldn't have been more different. I was placed in the Haverfield Dormitory on north campus with the Engineering Honors students. (Talk about a nerd herd.) All of the residents of this four-story building were white, apart from a fellow homie on the top floor and me, the little brown girl from India. I was confused when we were moving in, as I saw boys and girls on the same floor, and I innocently assumed that the boys were brothers helping their sisters out. It took me a few minutes to realize our floor was co-ed! Oh, the horror: boys and girls living next to each other! On top of that, my resident advisor was male too. I came from an all-girl, Catholic school, so this was quite a change.

Ideally, I would have had a chance to visit my dormitory, and learn more about what was in store for me before moving in, had the international students' orientation taken place. But orientation had been cancelled.

The International Students' Orientation was supposed to take place two weeks before move-in day and the start of classes. At the time I was living with Vikram. I was all excited for orientation day and my first visit to OSU. It was on a Tuesday morning in September. I was dressed and waiting at Vikram's house for him to take me to campus. Then the phone rang. "Niyati, I don't think you will have orientation today. Turn on the news." I rushed to the TV and turned it on. I was dumbstruck; a plane had crashed into one of the World Trade Center buildings in New York City. Confused, I said to Vikram, "This is tragic! I can't believe what I'm seeing. It's horrific. But I'm confused. Why would a plane crash in New York cancel orientation in Ohio?" He explained this was much bigger than a tragic accident—it was an attack on US soil. I thought he was being overzealous. Clearly something must have happened to the pilot, and this was some sort of accident. He told me to stay put, and that he would check with the university about orientation. I hung up and continued watching the news unfold live.

Another plane crashed into the second World Trade Center building. This was no accident. It was an attack on US soil, as Vikram said. I watched the Twin Towers turn to rubble. A plane crashed into the Pentagon, and another in a field in Pennsylvania. I thought about the time my father brought me and my sister to America in the 1990s. We had visited those towers. They were gone in what seemed like a blink of an eye.

That is why orientation got cancelled. Two weeks later I moved into the dorms. There was uneasiness on campus among the international students, nervousness about being in the US on a visa. *Are the visas going to get revoked? Are we going to get sent back? Will there be restrictions on what major we choose?* In fact we were questioned about which major we chose. Chemical and aeronautical engineering came under scrutiny. This was the lay of the land when I immigrated to the US. I had arrived just before 9/11, one of the most tumultuous times in US history. Some luck. Little did I know how much Ohio State would shape me as a person.

Fortunately, my experiences with my roommates and dorm friends were another story altogether. I was assigned a quad with three other girls. We had two rooms: one was a common area for our desks, and the other contained our bedroom with bunk beds, some closet space, and a bathroom. I'm not sure what my roommates thought, but honestly I felt it was luxurious. We had central air conditioning and heating, and our own bathroom. The biggest highlight for me was having running water 24-7! What luxury. And being in tight spaces reminded me of life in Mumbai, which always took place in close quarters.

But I didn't belong there, in that all-white building. I felt that I needed to be in an international dormitory. So, I spoke to the resident advisor, Justin, a pale, blonde, slender fellow doing his undergrad in pre-med. He told me that OSU required us to wait a week before changing dorms. "Fine, I'll wait that mandatory week, but I need you to help me relocate," I said. He said he would be happy to help me find another place, but that, in the meantime, I should make friends and give my roommates a chance. I decided to make an effort.

I started talking to Jennifer, a roommate from Upper Sandusky, Ohio. She was blonde, blue-eyed, and tall. At a staggering five feet, one inch, and eighty-eight pounds, I felt like I was in the land of the giants. Jen was warm and friendly, and I had a good feeling about her. She seemed genuine. I then introduced myself to the girls across the hall. The boys next door came over to speak to us. One of them said, "Hi, I'm Doug. I hear you're from India. I've been there on a mission trip." Doug with deep blue eyes—that was it. I had the biggest crush of my life, and everyone knew it. It's obvious when brown skin turns red that you're blushing. I was in love. This, my friends, is puppy love, innocent as can be.

The next day I knocked on Justin's door. "Hey, Justin, can I come in? I want to talk to you." He said sure, and closed the door behind him. "So, about that move request. Umm, let's put the relocation paperwork on hold." Justin had a big smile on his face. He was so happy that I felt welcome on his floor. "May I ask what changed?" I was honest (remember puppy love?). I sighed, and said, "Doug's blue eyes." Some amazing game there, right?

What followed might possibly have been the best four years of my life. Stop right there—you're thinking Doug and I dated? Yuck, no. But he ended up being a great friend to me, and I cherished our friendship.

Jen and I found that we really liked living with each other freshman year. She had just the right amount of OCD. She liked to keep our room clean and the bathroom smelling good. She was brilliant and studious, and her hard work paid off. We teamed up with Sarah from across the hall to be roommates sophomore year. The three of us got along great. We were never in each other's way and learned to live with and love each other. In fact, Jen and I ended up living together for all four years of undergrad.

We were good for each other. I stood up for her and protected her like a tigress. I couldn't stand to watch friends take advantage of her, and she knew that. We laughed together and cried together.

Seventeen years later Jen flew in from Minnesota to help me during radiation, leaving her family behind. Having Jen around was therapeutic. We talked about college days, our innocence, and the fun we had. She cooked, helped with errands, and entertained the kids. Jen has a heart of gold, as I've known since the day I met her.

• • •

In hindsight, attending Ohio State and living in the United States gave me an opportunity to change my narrative. I was no longer a fatherless daughter; I was just a girl from India, a geek who outsmarted most high school valedictorians. The magical thing about the US was that no one cared about your background or how much wealth your family had. I made close friends during undergrad, but most of them did not know I had lost my father. And if they did know, they didn't care. Ohio State gave me a chance to start fresh, and my four years there will forever be close to my heart.

At the beginning of senior year most of my engineering buddies and I started looking for jobs. Every fall there's a huge career fair on campus, and I was looking forward to making a good first impression through face-to-face contact, especially because, on paper, I was merely an immigrant looking for sponsorship. During the fair I stood in endless lines to talk to recruiters. Most were upfront with me, explaining that their company didn't sponsor H-1B visas. I got tired of giving my spiel only to hear that someone wouldn't sponsor me. So, I took a different approach; instead of exhausting myself trying to get an interview with a company that wouldn't hire me, *I* would ask the first question: "Do you sponsor H-1B visas?" This closed many doors, but I would always rather cut to the chase.

Eventually I got to the booth of a famous Fortune 500 company that makes the iconic yellow bulldozers. Let's call it Dozer Co. I asked a recruiter who was accepting resumes if they sponsored visas, and he said he didn't know the answer. He called on the head recruiter, Scott, to talk to me. Scott said, "We only sponsor H-1B for exceptional candidates." Without flinching, I replied, "Give me an opportunity to interview with you, and I'll prove that I'm an exceptional candidate." That's called "getting a foot in the door"—and it was all I needed to do. I got that job, and Dozer Co. sponsored my work visa.

Graduating with a job waiting for me was a great feeling and brought a big sense of relief. I had student loans to take care of, and I was ready to test out my engineering skills on the world. Graduation day was incredible. A class of 8,000 students marched into the Horseshoe, Ohio State University's iconic football stadium, all dressed in black gowns and black caps, our families looking on. The ceremony started with the national anthem and a dramatic hoisting of the American flag. Americans know how to instill patriotism, and I felt American that day. Part of me *was* American. My entire adulthood was spent in Ohio, and my education, my classmates, and my job were all American. I felt proud of the flag that day, because I saw a part of my identity in it.

Being in Ohio also put me close to the center of the Tamaskar hub. In the 1960s, when my great-uncle and his wife moved from India to England to Cleveland, Ohio became the focal point of my US-based family. This was the motivation behind me choosing to go to Ohio State for my undergraduate studies.

Thanksgiving in Ohio became a family tradition. No matter where we were, everyone made their annual trek to Cleveland. Most years there would be two houses full of adults and children. Manda *maushi* would cook up a feast. Every meal was served piping hot, fresh, and in abundance. It was an extravaganza! In all the years I've lived here, I have never once seen Manda *maushi* eat first. She is always making sure people's plates are filled, serving up hot chapatis, lentils, and more. I also can't remember the last time I ate *last*—guilty as charged! Between Vikram *dada* and me, we were always the first to eat.

Those four years of being at Ohio State, with Manda *maushi* as the center of the Tamaskar Universe, gave me a sense of security. I was far away from my immediate family, but I had family here who loved me and took care of their own. Those four years were also instrumental in establishing meaningful relationships with my cousins, uncles, and aunts, the same people who stood by me during my cancer journey.

It is hard for me now to look back and see how many years it took to redefine myself. With my identity as a daughter without a father and the stigma it carried in my culture, all I wanted was a new narrative. At each step of life's journey I added something new to my identity. My engineering degree, my first job, buying my own house, hiking Machu Picchu, getting married to Nuwan, and having two gorgeous babies were all part of my growth and my process for coming into my own.

That's not all that changed my identity. It evolved once again after my diagnosis, this time immediately and irreversibly. I am now also a cancer survivor. I need to use this new chapter of my life as a story of hope and courage. When my first cousin Prashant heard about my cancer diagnosis, this is what he texted me:

> Niyati you are the strongest person I know. Period. And you have been since you were a kid. There's no spouse better than Nuwan. Life has been unfairly cruel to you before, but it could never conquer you. I don't think I've ever told you how truly awestruck I am of your strength and vitality. Your spirit is indomitable.

Life had been unfairly cruel, and I needed someone to acknowledge that. So many people told me I was a warrior that I started to resent that word. What I needed was for someone to recognize the adversity I had faced in my life.

Destiny gave me a new narrative, one that included the role of cancer survivor. It included a fierce battle that would forever change me and my family, a battle that would claim a part of me and leave scars, both physical and emotional, that I will bear for life. Cancer invaded my body and my dreams, invaded my family.

This is my new narrative, one that I will convert into a story of hope, love, and triumph. I don't know how I'll get there, but what you're reading is a start.

13. PARADIGM SHIFT

**"We do not simply live in this universe.
The universe lives within us."**
— Neil deGrasse Tyson, *Astrophysics for People in a Hurry*

Any cancer survivor can you tell you the exact date, and possibly even the hour and minute, they got the dreadful news. Life after that phone call completely and irreversibly changes. Mine got split into two sections: life before cancer and life after diagnosis. I call them BC ("Before Cancer") and AD ("After Diagnosis"). Every event I remember is interpreted through this timeline. Because in BC, when we weren't staring death in the face, Nuwan and I had carefree, optimistic dispositions. But then again, no one at the age of thirty-four should be faced with their mortality, least of all a breastfeeding mother of two. People depended on me, little people, with precious lives.

In AD my perspective changed. Each hug I gave was genuine. Each time I said, "I love you," I didn't know if it would be my last. I poured my heart and soul into each thank you note. It might sound melodramatic, but that's how I felt, and it was authentic. I wasn't being fatalistic; I just wanted to be true to myself. Dare I say, I was vulnerable. Being vulnerable to the world by sharing my diagnosis made my skin crawl. But the alternative was not an option. I was not going to hide my cancer, and I was not ashamed. If this meant my friends, family, and colleagues would see me stagger or appear "emotional," so be it. It went against everything that I once stood for, but it needed to be this way.

And so I became the master of thank you notes. I handwrote more than fifty cards and letters during my cancer treatment. I wanted to fill the world with gratitude. Dozens of people came to help us during this fight, and I wanted each of them to know how much this meant to Nuwan and me. I had a debt to repay that I knew I never could, so I wrote. I profusely thanked everyone who touched our lives.

The relationships I had formed BC were put to the test, but the relationships I made AD became everlasting. Some of my closest friends from the BC period completely fell off the radar, stopped communicating, and kept their distance. Some cousins didn't respond to texts. Some colleagues pretended to be unaware of my situation. Some friends paid lip service to the idea of helping, and some stopped answering my calls altogether. No, seriously: one "friend" from the East Coast blocked me from his phone. It was pitiful. However, these humans formed a tiny and insignificant group of people that no longer means much to me, because a myriad of friends from my BC time came out of the woodwork to help, and new friends, forged in the AD phase, became part of my support system. My best friends from India texted and called incessantly. I got flowers and cards from so many people. Friendships were revived, tears were shed. I became close to friends with whom I had lost touch. More friendships were rekindled than broken. And that is the beauty of cancer.

Yes, there is beauty in cancer. Here's an example: My friend Katie made me a care package of lotions, teas, a warm blanket, slippers, and more. She wrote me a heartwarming letter. This is a snippet:

A lot of this will be hard but it will also generate some memories you will all cherish forever. I encourage you to write it all down, all that you can, as a form of therapy for yourself and memories for when you beat this. Take lots of pictures too. Your kids will want those to look back on when you talk about this with them as they grow up. You are a fighter by nature, your own best advocate and because of that... cancer had better watch its ass because it doesn't stand a chance against you. I'm not a bit worried, I am sorry its happening to you and I'll be here for you and your family the whole way. The days it gets harder to fight, the days you feel defeated or when self-pity is weighing on you like a wet blanket, or fatigue is too much to bear, call me, I've got your back.

And she really did have my back. There were numerous weekends during chemotherapy that Katie took Vihaan off our hands, taking him on playdates with her son and providing a huge relief. This gave me a three-to-four-hour break to rest. Whenever our friends took the kids off our hands it not only gave me time to recuperate, it helped us shelter them from the impact of my condition.

A big part of my growth came from reading a book called *Daring Greatly: How the Courage to be Vulnerable Transforms the Way We Live, Love, Parent and Lead* by Brené Brown. She starts the book with this quote from Theodore Roosevelt:

It is not the critic who counts; not the man who points out how the strong man stumbles, or where the doer of deeds could have done them better. The credit belongs to the man who is actually in the arena, whose face is marred by dust and sweat and blood; who strives valiantly; who errs, who comes short again and again, because there is no effort without error and shortcoming; but who does actually strive to do the deeds; who knows great enthusiasms, the great devotions; who spends himself in a worthy cause; who at the best knows in the end the triumph of high achievement, and who at the worst, if he fails, at least **fails while daring greatly**, so that his place shall never be with those cold and timid souls who neither know victory nor defeat.

I learned a lot about vulnerability from this book, which was given to me by Gary, my executive director. Gary stopped by one evening when we had Ravi *kaka* and Ujwala *kaku* over from Maryland. (Come to think of it, Gary has met my sister, husband, and kids, and an aunt and uncle. He is practically family.) Gary told my aunt and uncle how appreciated I am at work. I know that made them so proud.

If you haven't read *Daring Greatly*, I urge you to pick it up. Brené Brown rose to fame through her TEDx talk about vulnerability, and then national TED talks on the same topic. This book transformed the way I think about vulnerability. It taught me so much about myself and highlighted some cultural baggage I carry, baggage that I now know transcends cultures. I'll give you an example. In the book Brown talks about the concept of "foreboding joy." She asserts that joy is one of the hardest things to experience, because we don't let ourselves be vulnerable. Whenever things are going swimmingly well—kids are happy, job is stable, boss is satisfied, spouse is doting—we get nervous and think something terrible is about to happen and break up the party.

This mindset is just as common in India, where there's a saying: "Don't be too happy, or you will attract the evil eye." We call the evil eye *nazar* in India; In Sri Lanka it's called *es vaha*. The point is, we are cautioned to not be *too* happy. Isn't that ridiculous? All I want is for my children to be exceedingly happy. When Brown conducted her research, she asked people what experiences made them feel most vulnerable. The answers were overwhelmingly related to joy and love. It seems so counterintuitive, but I know the answers reflect how I feel. Brown lists some of the responses in the book, which include standing over your children while they're sleeping, having a baby, getting promoted, going into remission. When I came to this last one, I read it out loud. *Going into remission*—this couldn't be more accurate. When we were at the height of my cancer treatment, I was ready for battle. I didn't feel vulnerable or exposed. I needed help, but I was going to grab the bull by the horns. Now that I'm in remission I feel exposed; I'm scared. I don't want to be too happy, lest I attract the evil eye and relapse. I don't want *nazar*.

I am so grateful that Gary thought of me when he saw this book. The copy he gave me is even more special because of the note he handwrote inside the front cover:

> Dear Niyati,
>
> I hope you know just how much you are appreciated and loved by so many of us. Your journey this year has left me with every possible emotion: fear, sadness, hope, inspiration and triumphant joy...
>
> The title and review of this book caught my attention and I thought the timing of giving this to you might be good.
>
> I am thrilled that you are back and feeling good and will continue to pray for you as we also tackle exciting new opportunities at work.
>
> All the very best to you and your family—the best is yet to come!
>
> Gary

Relationships forged AD will undoubtedly be lifelong. I felt an indelible bond with my oncologist Stephanie and with my radiation oncologist Kevin. I wonder, do all cancer survivors feel this way? It isn't just that

I owe them my life, it's that they have seen me at my most vulnerable. They answered my questions and conducted excruciatingly long consults to ensure that I felt comfortable about the next steps. They listened to me without judgment, they saw me cry, they saw me bald, and they saw my mastectomy scars. What I cherished the most, though, was their empathy. Empathy is not about experiencing the identical hardship. It is about being able to relate to distress with your personal experience, a parallel experience. When my caregivers spoke about their life and their struggles, their compassion was palpable. They were vulnerable in return. And that is not easy.

After a cancer diagnosis, your perspective changes overnight. All of us know we are on this planet for a finite amount of time, yet we fool ourselves into believing that we will never get old. Newsflash: *old age is a privilege*!

Moments of clarity come from being under duress. For me this meant understanding how finite my life really was. Once when Catharine visited, I said, "Catharine, I feel like I'm living my life in fast-forward. I lost my father young. Dated Nuwan for a hot minute and knew with all certainty that he was my soulmate. Got pregnant both times in a heartbeat. Delivered one baby early. Both of my labors were fast. I feel the end, too, will come prematurely for me." Catharine said she had no doubt that I was going to live a long and healthy life. Bless her heart.

My mother, aunts, and everyone else around me keep telling me the same thing: "You will live a long life." During my treatment, speaking about my mortality was taboo. Back to the Indian belief in self-fulfilling prophecies. I was often met with responses like, "Don't think like that", or "Don't say that," or, "Believe in God," and all the positive affirmations known to man. Since when did we get so allergic to anything that's not dripping in positivity? I don't think it's pessimistic to talk about mortality when you're diagnosed with Stage 3, Grade 3 invasive ductile carcinoma—I think it's being realistic.

I was cognizant of the battle ahead of me from the get-go. The survival rates and percentages were thrown at us. There was—and there still is—a possibility that I won't be around in five years. While I am grateful for the best possible outcome after the pathological complete response (PCR), I have no idea of knowing what is in store for me in the future. Recurrence is a daunting possibility that plagues the minds of most, and possibly all cancer survivors. But I am forbidden to speak about it. Now that this is my new normal, reality is tinged with uncertainty. I am grateful that we beat the disease, and hopeful that it will not rear its ugly head ever again.

Another moment of clarity: truly realizing what's important to me. I call it the paradigm shift. I want to give my children a taste of experiences that have enriched me: being close to nature, sleeping under the stars, experiencing life in the wild. These are experiences that make me feel closer to the Almighty. I want my children to grow up with compassion, respect for nature, and love for animals. I want to teach my children what my grandmother Aaji taught me when I was little girl. She told me to recite this Sanskrit prayer in the morning before getting out of bed and putting my feet on the ground:

Samudra vasane devi parvatstana mandale,
Vishnupatni namas tubhyam padsparsam kshmasva me

Loosely translated: Mother Earth bears the burden of humanity, nourishes our body and soul, gives us air to breathe and water to drink. Before we callously step on Her we must ask for forgiveness, "Pardon me for touching you with my feet." (In Hinduism touching someone with the soles of your feet is considered disrespectful.) This prayer is the epitome of Hinduism, which is driven by seeing divinity in nature. Being close to nature is like being close to the Creator, hence we must show respect.

During chemotherapy, I remembered this prayer and recited it profusely, because the desperately toxic cocktail of drugs that were saving my tiny and insignificant life (cosmically speaking) had a tremendous impact on Mother Earth. Yes, even in this fragile state, I pondered my carbon footprint and the environmental impact that my treatment had. I was acutely aware that, as is true with some other drugs, chemotherapy agents were discovered in the most fundamental forms of nature: soil and plants. Adriamycin ("the Red Devil") is named after the Adriatic Sea; researchers at the Farmitalia pharmaceutical company found anticancer properties in soil microbes around the sea, leading to the development of the drug. Taxol, which caused a temporary but frightening neuropathy, comes from the bark of a Pacific Yew Tree. (You can find more information about these drugs on scientific websites or from the American Cancer Society. I'm not an expert, and I don't want to turn this book into a medical journal. But I wanted to highlight that the unique properties of certain kinds of soil and plants are what killed the cancer in my body.)

The only other time I experienced such a visceral change in perception was when I became a mother. When I was younger the universe seemed to revolve around me. I dreamed of decorating our office at home with a floor-to-ceiling-sized map of the world. I wanted to put pins on all the places we had visited: a pink pin for me and a blue one for Nuwan. I was proud of our travels. It seems so egotistical now. Today there's a world map the size of a wall in our house, but it's not in our office—it's in the kids' playroom. There are pink and blue stickers for all the places we've taken *the kids*. This small thing reflects a tremendous paradigm shift.

Parents say they'll do anything for their children, including take a bullet. This is me saying I'd go through cancer treatment, and even laugh for them.

14. WHAT NEXT?

"Your brain is you. Everything else is just plumbing and scaffolding."
— Bill Bryson, *The Body: A Guide for Occupants*

I finished radiation on October 3, 2018, seven months after my diagnosis. In most cancer centers across the United States, there's a tradition where patients who finish their treatment get to ring a bell three times. The bell says:

Ring this bell
Three times well
Its toll to clearly say,
My treatment's done
The course is run
And I am on my way.

That day I got to ring the bell. A few close friends showed up to watch me, and the oncologists and nurses on call came out of hiding and clapped for me. I hugged and kissed Nuwan, and we shared the most poignant moment of my life. My ordeal didn't end there, though. I will have follow-ups for a long time to come.

The post-bell buzz didn't last. So much had happened that, once it was all over, I checked out. I felt disoriented and helpless. I had nothing to fight against now, and instead of elation, I felt despair. It turns out I wasn't unique. In fact I learned that this is a common feeling among survivors who have recently finished treatment. Survivorship is harder than treatment.

I was in search of a purpose. An obvious calling seemed to be volunteering at the cancer center. You know me—no time to waste!—so on October 4, my first day of remission, I filled out a volunteer application form. The next day I interviewed with Volunteer Services about an open position that would have me take meal orders, restock supplies, and "make conversation." I texted the job description to Kevin saying, "Clearly you don't qualify; they need a conversationalist."

"You are poorly qualified for the job," he retorted. I love when people understand sarcasm. I dressed up in my work attire, which I hadn't worn in a couple months, for my interview.

To my surprise, the Volunteer Services representative informed me that there was a three-month waiting period after a patient completes cancer treatment. They explained that some past volunteers weren't able to transition from being a patient to becoming a provider. While I respected that limitations were in place based on past experiences, I did not understand them. More than a third of cancer patients are over the age of seventy-five, and more than half are between the ages of fifty and seventy-four. This makes the sample size of the survivor-turned-volunteer skewed. I'm thirty-five and have the energy and mental fortitude to help patients. What did they think, that I would be a blubbering mess while taking meal orders? Throughout treatment I was told that each person is different, and that everybody responds to treatment differently. I wanted them to treat my physical recovery and state of mind in the same way. I am not your average cancer patient. Let me rephrase: I am not your average *anything*. I am a survivor, who is fighting a hospital so that I can volunteer.

Nuwan supported me. He said it would be a great show of strength and a source of hope and courage for patients to see someone who has recently finished treatment back at the Cancer Center volunteering. I asked a cousin, who is also a young survivor and deeply involved in supporting breast cancer patients, about volunteering as a survivor. She told me that the Young Survival Coalition, a support group for young breast cancer survivors, has a six-month wait before someone who was in treatment can take up a leadership position. It seems this policy is practiced across the board. But I question why this waiting period has been put in place. The recovery period is based on data across what demographic of cancer patients? What do they expect happens in three or six months—that all memory of your cancer is erased?

These challenges showed me that being a young survivor is a unique experience. But I said my peace as Nuwan asked me to drop the idea of volunteering at the cancer center. He said there might be better opportunities for me to volunteer at work. He suggested starting a survivorship group at work. He was right, as he always is. (The only saving grace here will be if Nuwan doesn't read this book and know that I said this about him.)

What's next? That question continues to haunt me. On the last day of radiation Kevin said to me, "I'm giving you your life back." But it was a life I did not recognize. The humdrum work of engineering was something I wasn't ready for. I knew I needed some time off, to recover physically, and to give my soul time to heal now that we were done fighting. I granted myself a few weeks after the end of treatment before restarting work. I resumed going to the gym to regain strength. I spent a lot of time talking to Nuwan about how hollow I felt about returning to work. Nuwan reminded me that the electronic controls I designed for that 91-liter natural-gas engine are sitting in Nigeria right now, powering a hospital. He highlighted that what I do is important, and that engineers in my position get to make a difference in this world.

Next I reached out to Degaulle. He is often my go-to person when I need to be talked off the ledge. "When you walk into a room you inspire people," he told me. "When my girls look at you they think it's normal for an Indian girl to be an engineer. You are changing perceptions and breaking the mold, even without trying." This helped me refocus my attention on my engineering work.

I am lucky to be surrounded by people who encourage me. Vikram *dada* told me to take some time off after treatment, because once I returned to work, people would be looking at me to perform. And if I didn't, I would be left on the sidelines as the "poor cancer girl." Vikram always has my best interests in mind. He wanted to make sure that I took care of my physical body first, which would enable me to use my engineering and leadership abilities to the best of my capacity. I almost always listen to him, and he knows that. I respect and love him and Beena immensely. They have raised two incredible daughters. Arya has a heart of gold, and Maya is sweet as pie. Nuwan and I will be lucky if our children turn out half as well. But I digress. I digress, because this is how I felt at the end of treatment: disoriented. I was left with so many questions and a culmination of unresolved emotions. Remission left me feeling more isolated than the diagnosis. When I was diagnosed, a tidal wave of supporters showed up at my doorstep. Remission, on the other hand, is celebratory. An ending. And it brings with it the expectation that you'll go back to your "normal" life. But what is normal now? What I was feeling, and am still feeling, is a part of post-traumatic stress disorder (PTSD).

We all have our bad days. I have had my share of days tainted with self-doubt and loathing. I have battled with contempt—contempt for circumstances and contempt for people. I have been consumed by all that is toxic in the world. But there is an anchor that brings me back: my children, my husband, my family, and my friends; my cancer journey, and everyone who so selflessly volunteered to be part of it.

I often find myself wandering down memory lane. Sometimes the memories are of my two pregnancies and the miracle of childbirth. I still get goosebumps when I think about the moment my firstborn was placed on my chest. I feel exhilarated when I think of my daughter's birth and how perfect she was. Sometimes the memories are of the unique experiences Nuwan and I had during our travels. There is so much to be grateful for that all the pain fades into the background, at least temporarily.

Often, I run into people at work that who don't know about my journey. I am open about it, and I tell everyone. More often than not the conversation goes like this: "You got a haircut?" To which I say, "It wasn't a haircut—it was chemotherapy, and now the hair is growing back." I know it's cruel to just spring this on people, but I believe in not hiding my disease. A manager, who hadn't seen me for more than a year, bore the brunt of this revelation. He said he was touched by my story, and I told him that I'd forward the updates I had sent to the team during my treatment. He wrote this to me in response:

> Thank you so much for sharing this with me. The picture after ringing the bell choked me up a bit.
>
> I really don't have the words to articulate how much I'm in awe at how you handled such hardship. Like you said, cancer picked the wrong girl to mess with!!
>
> I am so glad I ran into you. Hearing your story really helped put things into perspective for me.
>
> It is my sincere hope and prayer that the cancer is behind you now and that you can put your full energy into your family. You are going to have an awesome story to tell your kids when

they get older and be such an inspiration and example of strength and determination for them.

Hope to see you around a bit more often now and hear how things are going.

Warm Regards,

Justin

I have a story to tell. This is my story. I want to inspire. The soul-searching will continue for decades to come. What is the purpose of our life on earth? Well, ask me in a decade. In the meantime, others may be able to provide hints. When I told Ghalila about my diagnosis, she offered to help with meals. "I will provide meals for you every Wednesday till your treatment is done," she asserted. I wanted to do a sanity check, "Ghalila, this is not a sprint; it's a marathon. The treatment will go on till the end of the year. I've been prescribed the deluxe package of cancer care: chemo, surgery and radiation. I can't have you making us meals every Wednesday."

Ghalila then told me something that changed my life: "Niyati, what is our purpose on Earth? I am a spiritual person, and I feel God has given me a purpose. It is to provide meals for you and your family in your time of need."

It was just that simple. Ghalila taught me that, when you are looking for a purpose, it doesn't have to be at a Peace-Corps-volunteer level. Sometimes the most important thing you can do is stay right in your backyard, helping a neighbor or a colleague.

When I talk about soul-searching and finding meaning, I don't think the answer is meditating in the Himalayas. The answer is all around us. It is amidst our friends and in our communities. If you can go volunteer in the Peace Corps, then great! My own dream is to someday volunteer for Engineers Without Borders. But Ghalila just simplified the whole search for meaning. Pulled from the jaws of death, I had been given a second chance. How would I use this gift? I had come face-to-face with my mortality. I was a changed person, and I'm now acutely aware of our limited time on earth. I feel a sense of urgency in the things I do. I will spend the rest of my life giving back and paying it forward. I owe this to the universe.

I continue to seek tranquility. I cherish my children. I believe in the miracle of life. I miss my pregnancies. I yearn for the time when I was breastfeeding. I mourn my breasts. I love Nuwan. *I love Nuwan.*

At times it felt unbearable, but I was not about to give up the fight for my life. I fought for my children, and I fought for my husband. I fought for my mother, and I fought for my sister. *I fought for me.* This was not going to be my final chapter. I wouldn't let it.

ACKNOWLEDGMENTS

D r. Sanjeevani Tamaskar, my mother: you are the reason I write. Your love gives me the confidence to take on the world. Aai, thank you for encouraging all of my wild endeavors and for always having my back.

To my father, Rajendra Tamaskar: I'm nothing without you. You are the fire in my soul. I am everything because of you.

Asya Blue, my talented cover designer: thank you for beautifully capturing the ethos of my writing through illustration and color.

Adam Rosen, my editor: thank you for helping an engineer attempt to become an author. Go Bucks!

For enabling the strong women of our family to come help me, I'd like to thank the husbands: Adam, Deepak, Prashant, and Kamlesh. You took care of everything on the home front and encouraged me to fight on.

For sending nutritious, home-cooked foods, rich in iron and protein and made from the best quality ingredients, I would like to thank Mummy, Kamlesh's mother.

For leaving Elsa behind and coming to help during radiation, I would like to thank Sarika. You are wise beyond your years.

Vikrant: Thank you for your thorough emails, phone calls, research on second opinions, and concern at every step of the treatment.

For visiting us and cooking me delicious meals, I want to thank Shubhu *maushi*. Nuwan and I enjoyed your stay.

For babysitting Aarini every Saturday for weeks during chemo, I would like to thank Joan, Will, and their children.

For taking a keen interest in my recovery, removing barriers from our life, and delivering meals post-surgery, I would like to thank Cathy.

A huge thank you to PSBU—there's no better place to work.

For never giving up on me, I would like to thank Yohan, Krupali, Tasneem, Neha, and Ashok.

To Konstantin and Anastasia: I was humbled when you, without hesitation, told me that we were most welcome to stay at your place in Seattle if there were any treatment options exclusive to the Pacific Northwest. The care packages you sent me during chemotherapy, and texts and phone calls, were a source of strength. *Hindi Russi bhai bhai!*

For putting together an exhaustive binder full of information within forty-eight hours of my diagnosis, I would like to thank our friends Randy and Stephanie. The Johnson family made us care packages, checked in on me, and volunteered for hospital runs and consults while giving us the space we needed. Thank you for answering my 3 a.m. phone calls.

For making me *dosa* and the cappuccino of champions before each of my surgeries, I would like to thank Raj and Archana. Vihaan spent several Sundays at your place, playing for hours. I cannot describe the relief I felt when we could remove Vihaan and Aarini from the house of cancer.

To my peeps at the gym, Jenny and Tracy: You have been a pillar of support to me through this journey.

A big "thank you" to our neighbor Siri for delivering meals every Sunday, and for taking Vihaan out on playdates.

For being good neighbors even after moving 300 miles away, to Emily, Firas, Cheri, and Rick: Thank you for the flowers, cards, hats, and texts.

A tip of the hat to our neighbors in Leamington, the Power family: Thank you for the support during my treatment and for offering to fly across the pond to come help us.

For checking on my cardiac health, giving me company at the Cancer Center, and more, I would like to thank Nandu. You have been a huge support to us during this trying period.

For loving on Aarini and watching the kids on several weekends, I would like to thank Jenny and Cierra.

For wrapping me in toasty blankets, I would like to thank the oncology nurses at CRH.

For painstakingly ensuring we got the breath-hold technique right every single time, I would like to thank the radiation therapists at CRH.

If you're thinking to yourself, *I was a huge part of Niyati's cancer journey— where's my name?* Read the book! If you're not in the back, it's probably because you're part of the story.

ABOUT THE AUTHOR

Niyati Tamaskar is an advocate for women in technology and engineering. She has spent her professional career developing electronic controls for a variety of machine applications and natural gas engines. She works as a technology planner, managing programs related to sustainability and energy security. Her passion for engineering extends to her work as regional leader of Center for Women in Technology (CWiT) North America. She promotes STEM education and strives to prioritize engineering careers among minorities.

When Niyati was diagnosed with breast cancer, she realized that she was a statistical outlier, because this disease only occurs in 3% of lactating women. As an Indian, she also realized the all-too-common truth that people with serious illness are often shunned, and that discussing a disease like cancer is taboo. She chose not to be silent and challenged the cultural norm by writing this memoir. All proceeds of the book are donated to the American Cancer Society. Her 2020 TEDxBloomington talk on cultural bias and stigma associated with cancer was widely recognized.

Niyati immigrated to the United States from India in 2001. Currently, she lives in Columbus, Indiana, with her husband and their two children. Her hobbies include cooking and traveling the world. She is passionate about connecting with people through her writing. You can read more about her at bombaybelle.wordpress.com

DISCUSSION GUIDE

You're invited to enhance your book club, support group, or gathering of friends with this discussion guide. This page may be reproduced and shared for these educational purposes only. (A copyright applies to the rest of the book.)

Q1. Being honest and open about your concerns with your doctor can be difficult. Based on the author's story and your own experience, how do you foresee navigating such conversations?

Q2. Do you have a friend or loved one who has been affected by cancer? To the extent that you feel comfortable discussing it, how did you hear about their diagnosis? If you received your own diagnosis, how did you choose to share the news, if at all, with others?

Q3. Prior to reading this book, did you believe that showing emotion was a sign of weakness? Do you perceive it differently today? If so, how?

Q4. The author relied on support from people who lived nearby. How would you describe your interactions with your own neighbors?

Q5. If you could call on one person for nonjudgmental support, who would it be?

Q6. Taboos exist in every culture. Can you describe some that you are familiar with in your culture(s) of origin, or perhaps a taboo that you've observed when moving within other cultures?

Q7. Was there a situation in the book that made you laugh out loud? Do share with your discussion group!

Q8. Why do you think the author introduced the chapter "Fire in My Soul" so late in the book? Did this chapter help you to gain insight into her story of cancer treatment?

Q9. Victim blaming occurs when individuals are held completely or partially responsible for harm that occurs to them in their lives. Victim blaming comes in many forms. Have you witnessed or experienced this phenomenon? What was the impact, either on you personally or on a social level?

Q10. If you could give the author one piece of advice, what would it be?

The author can be reached through her website:
bombaybelle.wordpress.com